CLOSER
TO THE
EDGE

ALSO BY THIS AUTHOR

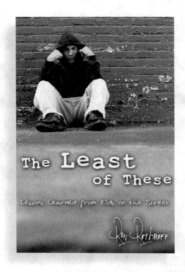

Through concrete detail, current statistics, and insights from more than 25 years living among and ministering globally to youth mired in tough and dangerous street life, Ron Ruthruff provides a tried model for serving not only troubled youth but others as well.

His stories compel us to reach the least, the last, and the lost, and to appreciate what they can teach us as well. Readers will hear the voice of Job from the hospital bed of a heroin addict, read the story of Mark 5 from the perspective of an "untouchable" in an orphanage in Bombay, India, and discover that the children who sit on our city streets around the world are not just a problem to be solved, but have the potential to become some of our greatest teachers in both their depravity and their dependence on God.

The Least of These
Lessons Learned from Kids on the Street

RON RUTHRUFF

ISBN-13: 978-1-59669-272-5
N104135 • $19.99

To learn more, visit NewHopePublishers.com.

CLOSER TO THE EDGE

WALKING WITH JESUS FOR THE WORLD'S SAKE

RON RUTHRUFF

NEW HOPE®
PUBLISHERS
Gospel-Centered. Missions-Driven.

BIRMINGHAM, ALABAMA

New Hope® Publishers
P. O. Box 12065
Birmingham, AL 35202-2065
NewHopePublishers.com
New Hope Publishers is a division of WMU®.

New Hope Publishers serves its authors as they express their views, which may not express the views of the publisher.

Library of Congress Control Number: 2015951047

ISBN-10: 1-59669-441-6
ISBN-13: 978-1-59669-441-5

N154119 • 1215 • 2M1

DEDICATION

This work is dedicated to my sons, Ben and Clayton. Your questions, your challenges, your unwillingness to accept a spirituality that is not lived out has helped shape my thinking for this work.

CONTENTS

ACKNOWLEDGMENTS

Julie Mullins, my dear friend and first reader on this project: thank you for your editorial wisdom and your amazing ability to hear my voice through all my attempts to write this book.

The Street Psalms Community, in which I am ordained to serve, my brothers and sisters who constantly live the stories that I tell: you put the *practical* in practical theology! The story of God you proclaim — it is truly good news in hard places.

Tuesday night church, some of you call me *Pastor*, others *Pops*, and to some I am *Doc*: you have been the most intimate community I have ever broken bread with. You taught me how to set a bigger table.

The 98118 zip code that has been our home for 26 years: I have seen the face of God in your faces.

The Seattle School of Theology and Psychology faculty, staff, and students: you have given me a place to give away all that I have been given.

And my friends at New Hope Publishers for letting me push the theological envelope for the world's sake.

To my best friend Linda, who loves me enough, after 29 years of marriage, to continue to call me to live all I teach.

INTRODUCTION

When I was young, I lived in my imagination. My mother raised me by herself and she was wonderful. I lived in my imagination because my playmates were few and infrequent. This led to many imaginary friends, like Pete and Frank. They were two of my closest buddies and were willing to reenact Civil War battles, in which we would fight for the Union cause of freedom, and Vietnam skirmishes that would always end in our being saved or saving the buddy next to us. Frank and Pete were always faithful, brave friends, and I could not have imagined any better.

My mother was a courageous, strong woman who was terrified that something would happen to her only son, the only living memory of her husband, my father, who died too early and left his wife to protect her little boy. I was three years old and my sisters were grown when this crisis hit my family. It's also when I started living in my imagination because risk was to be avoided at all cost. My mother worked a lot, and fear became a guiding force that babysat me in her absence.

When I was probably five or six, my mother's sister Erma and her husband Frank visited us from Michigan. My Aunt Erma was beautiful in a 1940s Midwest sort of way, and Uncle Frank was big and strong and kind, like you would expect a man from Iowa to be.

We took a few day trips, one to Diablo Dam. I still remember it was a beautiful spring Washington day. I remember what I wore because it was what I always wore: a gray felt cowboy hat, blue jean jacket and jeans, a two-gun toy belt, and suede cowboy boots. My Uncle Bill always called me "Tex" because little Ronnie always wore six-guns and boots. I wore those boots until I wore a hole in the sole the size of a 50-cent piece.

The moment that stands out in my mind that day happened in the parking lot, or maybe at a viewpoint near the dam. I was being pretty squirrely. The two-hour drive in the back of my mother's 1968 Dodge Dart had almost paralyzed me, and the minute I stepped out of the car, I needed to get the wiggles out. With a burst of energy, I ran toward the lake that lay below the dam overshadowing the parking lot. As I galloped to the edge of the overhang, my big Uncle Frank reached out and grabbed my jacket with a kind but cautious "be careful, Tex" grab. I don't know if I was in imminent danger. I don't know how far the drop or how deep the water was, and I don't know how many times my mother told the story afterward, but it was enough that I soon lost count.

According to her, the drop was deadly and the white water tumultuous, and as the gravel kicked away from my boot, it tumbled over the edge like feathers being dumped from a pillow. My life had been miraculously spared that day, and my mother was spared the horror of losing both men in her life. She never mentioned my Uncle Frank as she retold me the story, the strong hand that caught me regardless of how rambunctious I happened to be. My mother felt it was her job to keep me safe and vigilant and on the straight and narrow, by any means necessary. Lesson learned. Do not get too close to the edge. To my mom, this was the principle directing her life and experience of faith: getting it right, staying away from the edge and as far away from the world as possible. In many ways, if I am honest with myself, much of my wounding and my strength is tied to this story. It is also the catalyst for writing this book.

Now, as I look back, I have to admit much of what I write is a reflection on places and people that have revealed to me faith, hope, and love in places where brokenness abounds and — as crazy as it sounds — where grace is far more obvious. As I truly rub elbows with folks on the train, in my neighborhood, and in some amazing places I will never totally understand, I see in our joy the story of God's desire to be with us. I also see in our pain — what we call injustice — the absence of God. But that strange absence is making room for something divine.

So I invite you to read, not the book but the places in your own life where, in simply living life in all its complicated mess with other human beings, you see God. And when you see the absence of God, in humility declare the way things are and the way things are supposed to be.

As you walk with me through the pages of this book, I encourage you to let the place where you live reveal the best and the worst in you. I ask you to resist the impulse to fix things too fast, rather, wait! Wait with those who are suffering. The most caring thing you could do in some instances is to declare your inability to help and state that life is indeed hard and easy answers are usually wrong. I challenge you to look for the kingdom of God in strange and awkward places; it usually grows as something that doesn't look all that heavenly. Trust that you are being sent into the world, and believe that what the world needs are acts of mercy, systems of justice, and communities that have the courage to set bigger tables. Remember, the journey we are invited on is a journey where life dies when we hold too tightly and blossoms when we let go.

The real question of the book is, how far are we willing to go in this walk with Jesus? Are we willing to admit to others that we too have faced wilderness, desert, and exile? Do we walk into death thinking that new life is formed there? This is a ridiculous invitation unless you really believe — I mean really believe — that losing your life is the only way to find it and that resurrection is real. A resurrection that does not push us into the afterlife but, rather, back into the world with confidence, courage, fear, and trembling to live our lives honestly for the world's sake. This resurrection causes us to trust in the power of grace, mercy, compassion, and justice, believing that this journey is not just for the world's sake, but in this walk, we save our own lives as well. We walk to reveal that the love of God, lived through Jesus, sustains us even in death!

With all respect to my dear mother, who did what she thought was right to protect me, it is my hope to live a little closer to the edge. To learn to live as an honest, just, and merciful human being. I believe that the story of Jesus is the story of a God who risks everything and invites us to do the same. It is with all faith and assurance in this holy and human story that I take a step a little closer to the edge, maybe uncomfortably so for some. My desire is to consider how good news calls us to love radically and, as an act of deep trust in the story of God, living a bit more recklessly for the sake of the world. Here's to walking a little closer to the edge and trusting that a Hand has already caught me.

CHAPTER 1

THE CITY IS MY TEACHER, THE WORLD MY CLASSROOM

I love the city. And I mean more than just the physical place. I mean all the ways the urban landscape serves as a metaphor —a diverse sociological construct, filled with different opinions, values, faces, and symbols. Sometimes cities can feel like the wilderness, the desert, or similar places of exile. Cities can create disorientation. I have learned to love the complexity of urban environments. Over the past 15 years, I have had the incredible privilege of traveling frequently and building friendships with great people in great cities. Teaching has taken me to Guatemala City, Ho Chi Minh City, Mumbai, Nairobi, Phnom Penh, Santo Domingo, and countless cities across the United States. I get to work with colleagues who are local indigenous leaders, and who have been gracious enough to share their knowledge with me. Being with them has allowed me to see cities from new and unexpected perspectives.[1]

There is neither Jew nor Gentile, neither slave nor free,
nor is there male and female, for you are all one in Christ
Jesus. —GALATIANS 3:28

Here in Galatians, Paul makes a radical statement on justice: no longer do race, gender, or economic status dictate how we relate to each other. In this new kingdom, there is no division. But while he proclaims this to be true "in Christ," many who are involved in the struggle for justice today would say this is still an unrealized hope. If you surveyed one hundred people, you would get vastly different responses about how close we are to living out this amazing vision: no more divisions, a kingdom in which each person is treated as an equal participant. How we get there is complicated. It will take some combination of corporate responsibility and individual transformation. To be honest, I don't know exactly how we'll get there. But I have learned a little about where we might want to start.

I don't think we can do justice properly without admitting the effects of class, gender, sexual identity, and ethnicity on our shared experience. I don't think we can love our neighbor unless we admit that what Paul hopes for seems to be a long way off. Each of us, me included, must be willing to look deeply at the possible limits of our own perspectives and the psychosocial assumptions that come with our position in society. So this is my confession: I am a white, heterosexual male—the trinity of privilege—and I believe that this gives me a certain amount of access in our culture, access that women, people of color, those with a disability, and those whose sexual orientation is different than mine do not have. My location also creates blind spots, hiding entire worlds that I just can't see. I keep asking myself the questions: How do my markers of identity impact how I am perceived and how I perceive the world? What does it mean to fight for justice and love the world when we all come from such different places? How do we honestly explore the social collateral that some of us have been given and some of us have been denied? How do we intentionally spend this currency in the right places and in the right way?

This does not mean that if you are not a white, heterosexual male you don't need to ask these same questions. All of us need to ask how our social locations create psychological and sociological lenses through which we look at the world. These lenses shape our identities and the questions we ask. They shape how we make meaning in our lives and how we are able, or not able, to live with each other. So, how do we go about rethinking our starting points as we try to move toward Paul's vision of a community in which women and men and all cultural groups are treated fairly and with justice?

I've learned that I love large populations of different people trying (sometimes) to learn to live with each other. I love having access to a variety of foods, lifestyles, and neighborhoods. I love big public libraries, public parks, and public transportation. I love the vibrant art and music scenes that accompany this complexity. I love a lot of cities. Philadelphia is my favorite East Coast city — it has the architecture of Boston and the attitude of New York. But, most of all, I love Seattle.

My wife, Linda, and I love walking through our city, and our neighborhood is an especially great place to walk. I've been told that our zip code is one of the most diverse in the United States. I am sure there are neighborhoods

///

Let the otherness of your community reveal your blind spots.

**

in New York City and elsewhere that might take issue with this claim. But the 98118 has been my home for 25 years, and I can vouch for its diversity. Our neighborhood has synagogues, mosques, temples, and Bible-believing churches all within walking distance of each other. Census reports show Rainier Valley is almost exactly one-third white, one-third black, and one-third Asian. But even this description is a broad generalization that misses the diversity of our community. Some 60 languages are spoken here, and the terms *black* and *Asian* don't accurately represent the wide-ranging ethnicities that get lumped into these categories.[2] And while *white* implies Protestant and Catholic, it also includes a large Jewish community, of which many members walk to a variety of synagogues around our neighborhood.

But here's the main reason I love the city: I love what it teaches me, and even what it reveals in me. *Transcendence* is a theological term that means God is "other" or different from us. I have learned so much about this theological concept by living, working, playing, and worshiping in this community. I learn about the otherness of God from the different faces in my neighborhood. Cities, in all their diversity, begin to show me that my perspective is simply that: my perspective.

As John Rennie Short has observed in his book, *The Urban Order: An Introduction to Cities, Culture, and Power,*

> They (cities) are a mirror of our societies, a part of our economy, an element of our environments. But above all else they are a measure of our ability to live with each other. When we examine our cities, we examine ourselves.

///
White flight has actually resulted in broken communities in the suburbs.
**

The 98118 neighborhood and the cities around the world that I have visited have served as the most incredible classrooms, and the people I have met have been my most valued teachers. Short says that cities measure our ability to live with each other. I think at the heart of this observation is a challenge to let the place where you feel called to do justice teach you and shape you. Let this place measure your ability to live with, to be in community with, the other. Let the otherness of your community reveal your blind spots. Let place inform how you do your helping. When Short claims that when we examine the city, we examine ourselves, he means that the city, in all its complexity and diversity, presents us with an opportunity. Our encounters with those we think of as "other" can reveal things about ourselves, individually and collectively. I would argue that cities teach us the best and the worst about ourselves, and that this helps us move toward a place of justice.

Many of us who come from a place of power, privilege, and choice — or our families in generations past — have moved away from places that are economically and ethnically diverse to places that are far more familiar and comfortable. This is human nature; it seems to be the covert American dream. People have moved for safety, comfort, and familiarity since the beginning of time. In their comprehensive book *Urban Ministry: The Kingdom, The City and The People of God*, authors Harvie M. Conn and Manuel Ortiz describe how London's evangelicals created the suburban ideal of the English-speaking world in the late eighteenth and early nineteenth centuries: "Here moral purity could be safeguarded in class isolation"

///

If cities tell us a little about our ability to live with each other, some of it is bad news. Heterogeneous environments can expose things that some of us are simply blind to.

\\\

from the danger, cruelty, profane language, and immorality of urban London as well as people suffering on its streets.

For some, avoiding the city has been a moral imperative. But this is no guarantee of safety, security, or healthy families and communities.

In his book about adolescents growing up in a new America in the 1990s, *Cold New World: Growing Up in a Harder Country*, William Finnegan reports on a suburb in Los Angeles (LA) County, finding that white flight has actually resulted in broken communities in the suburbs. Parents who fled the diversity and perceived danger of LA ended up traveling long distances to work, leaving their children with little afterschool supervision or activities and support. Resistant to high taxes in the same community, once in the suburbs, families resisted taxes that would support schools, roads, and human services. As a result of what one might call a disregard for place, the children of these families struggled to graduate from high school, young people had limited access to college, and many of these kids, lacking community and connection, formed gangs. The outcome was the same as the neighborhoods they fled. Without support and infrastructure, neighborhoods erode and kids lose their way, regardless of ethnicity or geographical location.[3]

My encouragement to those turn-of-the-century London evangelicals and to city-fleeing communities in southern California is to have the courage to ask: What would have happened if you had stayed? What if we all chose to stay close to the intersections where people who are economically, ethnically, and religiously different live, play, and work? What if we resisted the impulse to dive back into the familiar and instead reentered, with curiosity, places that can be disorienting, along the way acknowledging that disorientation might be a crucial step in spiritual and social growth? We must be willing not to run away but be open to what a place can reveal about us and our relationships to each other.

The reason I live in the 98118 is because I need this neighborhood far more than it needs me. The city — the complex, multicultural, multiethnic, sexually diverse city — teaches me. It teaches me the best and the worst about myself. And it can teach me something about justice, something about being Christian, and something about living rightly in the world.

THE WORST ABOUT MYSELF

We don't have to look too far back in our history or too far from home to see what Short is attempting to draw our attention to. During the writing of this manuscript, a suburb of St. Louis exploded in demonstrations after a police officer shot multiple times and killed an unarmed 18-year-old African-American man. The police officer who shot and killed him is part of a majority white police precinct serving a majority black suburb. Regardless of whether one interprets the killing as racially motivated or not — an act of fear or simply an unjust act — the larger question is: Why do Americans from different communities see the event so differently? I think the deep schism in American culture over race issues speaks to how differently one experiences our country depending on the color of one's skin. In 1992, riots broke out in Los Angeles after four officers were acquitted in the beating death of Rodney King. In New Orleans in 2005, flood-waters caused a city to scatter in chaos; it was the poor and margin-alized who didn't have the resources to escape and, in many cases, have yet to recover. In 2010, a stop-and-frisk law implemented by the New York Police department led to 600,000 incidents of stop and frisk, an action designed to confront criminal activity. Ninety per-cent of those targeted were African American or Latino, but less than 15 percent of these stop-and-frisk events were initiated by any sort of "criminal activity."[4]

If cities tell us a little about our ability to live with each other, some of it is bad news. Heterogeneous environments can expose things that some of us are simply blind to. In his stirring book on Martin Luther King, *I May Not Get There With You: The True Martin Luther King, Jr.*, Michael Eric Dyson divides the King movement into before-Chicago and after-death, meaning that King and his constituents understood the overt racism of the South, but hit some snags and stalled (a kind of death) when they had to negotiate the covert racism of northern cities such as Chicago. Chicago's hidden codes and unwritten rules proved to be a significant challenge to the movement.

In my own neighborhood, I have benefited from the legacy of some of those hidden codes directly—specifically, the practice of redlining neighborhoods. Redlining is an illegal banking practice (one that Dyson alludes to in his book) in which financial institutions tar-get communities that are poor, nonwhite "risky" neighborhoods and limit the home or business loans they will offer, either denying loans or charging more for poor communities of color. Redlining can also include blocking the building of supermarkets, hospitals, and other public services. Because redlining is illegal, sometimes reparations are made where the practice has been exposed. Linda and I were able to increase our loan amount because we were willing to purchase in a formerly redlined neighborhood.

The hidden codes dividing cities along race and class lines don't end there. As we moved into the Rainier Valley neighborhood as guests some 25 years ago, and now as I have grown in my friendships, taken the train, shopped, and walked in our neighborhood, the city has exposed something else to me. Even though drug use — and the crime that accompanies it — seems to cross ethnic and economic lines in the Valley, it always seems like the young men in my community who who have black or brown skin go to jail more often and serve more time for drug crimes. I can't tell you how many times I have heard the stories of young men of color between the ages of twenty and thirty sitting in jail waiting for a trial and then, regardless of their culpability, entering a guilty plea. Word on the street is that sometimes if you plead guilty, you do less time than if you plead not guilty, get assigned a public defender, and wait for a trial. Reading Michelle Alexander's *The New Jim Crow: Mass Incarceration in the Age of Colorblindness*, I began to feel less crazy, and as though my gut observations about my neighborhood were not just about my predisposed beliefs about race in America. Alexander argues that the targeting of men of color during the war on drugs constituted yet another social system, such as the old Jim Crow laws of the post-Civil War South, to paralyze or hold captive certain segments of the population.

///

Cities expose this disconnect — the very disconnect that makes race and justice so difficult to talk about.

\\\

Bakari Kitwana seems to concur with Alexander's conclusions in his book, *The Hip Hop Generation: Young Blacks and the Crisis in African-American Culture,* when he says that in many states,

> Offenders convicted of crimes involving as little as five grams of crack cocaine receive a minimum five years in prison. For a powder cocaine offender to receive a similar sentence, the crime would have to involve nearly one hundred times that amount.

I learned from my neighborhood that if the war on drugs had really been about ending the distribution of forbidden substances, two police could have posted themselves in front of any legal drug paraphernalia shop in any college town in America and been just as successful. But the arrests were disproportionately young, black, and male.

Kitwana states that one-third of all black men between the ages of twenty and twenty-nine are incarcerated, on probation, or on parole. Blacks nationally make up 13 percent of monthly drug users; whites are 74 percent of illegal drug users. Yet, Kitwana goes on to say that according to the national Criminal Justice Commission, 74 percent of all those sentenced to prison for drug charges are black. The legacy of the war on drugs is alive and well. What is so amazing to me is that if I quote these stats in a classroom of students who come from mostly white communities, they are usually shocked. But for young people in my neighborhood, this is a daily reality, simply old news. Cities expose this disconnect — the very disconnect that makes race and justice so difficult to talk about.

I would hope that as I present these observations, we would resist the impulse to blame individuals and instead step back to ask a much bigger question. If certain behaviors seem to be prevalent in certain places among certain people — if Kitwana and Alexander are correct — then what are the larger societal processes at work? Cities can't hide these processes because we are constantly brushing shoulders with people who are effected by them in different ways. The question is, are we willing to be in conversation with each other? Cities, and, specifically, diverse communities, begin to expose us to clues, showing us what these large societal processes might be. My neighborhood has told me that racism, classism, and xenophobia still exist, and no matter how much we believe there is neither slave nor free, we are not there yet. We must be willing to create the kind of border-crossing relationships that help us explore why we all see justice so differently.

The problem is that we just don't have enough proximity to each other to start the kinds of conversations that help us learn why we all see justice differently. This inability to understand is the paralyzing effect of a lack of cross-border relationships. We don't shop together, go to school together, play together, let alone go to church together. How do we expect to know each other?[5]

Proximity, we will learn from the Good Samaritan, is the first step in loving a world that is different than us. The question is, are we willing to truly live our lives in the public square and embrace all that means? Some of us love public radio; public television is great. Some might even embrace public transportation. But things get more complicated when we think about public education, public health, and most of us avoid public bathrooms. My question is, for the sake of the world, how willing are we to live our lives in public?

THE BEST ABOUT US

Cities have certainly taught me to examine the worst in me, and in us. The insidiousness of poverty and racism hovers over the 98118. But cities have also told me about the very best in us.

Soon after the tragedy of September 11, 2001, I found myself in a 7-Eleven late one evening. The man behind the counter appeared to be of Middle Eastern descent. A few of us customers were wandering around the store for random items. A man in a suit got out of a very nice car and walked in the store. The doorbell had barely stopped ringing when the man demanded a cup for a soft drink. As two or three of us began to gather around the register, he raised his voice. He told the 7-Eleven employee to throw the cup away; the cashier had allegedly touched the inside of it. The man wasn't done. He began expressing his outrage at "these people" who were taking away American jobs. The well-dressed man didn't appear as though he needed a job at 7-Eleven.

Now he was at top decibel. He shouted that "after what just happened"—I assumed he was talking about 9/11—"these people shouldn't even be here." He was preaching to all of us now. The 7-Eleven employee stood there quietly. Then, a big construction worker, still in his hardhat and orange vest, had heard enough: "Wait a minute, this man's parents had just as big a dream for him as your parents had for you. He's just as American as any of us! So if you can't be served by him, you might as well leave."

The rebuttal froze the ranting, angry man. He had never expected opposition. For what felt like about half an hour, silence fell over 7-Eleven. All you could hear was the Kenny G track playing in the background. Then the man in the suit, without a word, walked out. The construction worker looked at the 7-Eleven employee, apologized, then said something I will never forget: "It's not sup-posed to be like that. I had to say something." It was the strangest time I ever spent in a 7-Eleven. I'm sure we all have stories of a simple bystander doing something unsolicited and amazing in public. In a little convenience store, in the mix of a bunch of different people, I got a glimpse of not only our worst, but our best.

///

When my boys were in middle school, they both played sports. Ben played basketball and Clayton played Ultimate Frisbee. One year, Ramadan, the Muslim month of fasting, fell during Ultimate Frisbee season. Quite a few Muslim kids played on the Frisbee team, and because Muslims fast from sunup to sundown, morning matches were always best. A group of Muslim parents always came to the game and were kind but distant. I introduced myself, but that was about it. One week in between Saturday games, Clayton asked why he never fasted. Of course, Linda told him he was a growing boy who, at thirteen, didn't need to fast. He went on to explain that he watched the Muslim kids fast, and he was just as serious about his faith, and basically demanded that we allow him to incorporate the spiritual discipline into his routine. That Saturday, I had a knot in my stomach. I kept wondering why I felt impelled to say something to the other parents, and so nervous about what seemed like such a small way of extending myself. When we all arrived at the Ultimate Frisbee field and I heard a voice inside me tell me clearly what I needed to do, it didn't help my anxiety — it exasperated it. So, with a couple of deep breaths, I walked up to the group of Muslim men. I told them about Clayton's request. "I just wanted to tell you all thank you," I said awkwardly. "Somehow your faith is helping my son grow in his." That was it. They smiled politely and told me I was welcome, and I walked away. Maybe this was one of those moments where I realized in yet another way that we all need each other. Or maybe it was simply a moment where I wasn't the expert trying to give advice or be helpful, and it felt strange and good. I still don't know what it means, but I liked it.

From the time my sons were in elementary school, they were fascinated by all the expressions of spirituality in our neighborhood. There was the fasting during Ramadan, and every Saturday we would see Jewish families honoring the Sabbath by walking to synagogue. When Ben was nine and Clayton was six, they began to ask as we read Bible stories at bedtime, "Why can't we tell our story of God to our friends?" Now, I need to add a little disclaimer. This was a profoundly nonevangelical request. The boys had no issue with the other kids' stories, and conversion wasn't part of either of their vocabularies. This was, in my fatherly evaluation, a simple request: let's tell our friends about the stories that teach us about God and give us hope. As the divine providence of God would have it, the church we were attending was launching summer Backyard Bible Clubs. This could have been the spark that ignited Ben and Clayton's desire to tell their story of God. So we committed ourselves to one week of Backyard Bible Club.

We did your standard stuff, using countless garbage bags to build — with the help of a big fan — the belly of a whale that seated about 15 kids for the story of Jonah. My

> ///
> *If we can refuse the impulse to run back to what is familiar and comfortable, cities and other places of diversity can tell us the best and the worst about ourselves, and a little about doing justice in the world.*
> \\\

best friend, Hala, was recruited as Zacchaeus, because Hala is about five feet six inches tall. We gathered strawberry baskets for cages for Daniel and the lion's den, and lots of cotton balls for sheep, and the week went by with fewer challenges than I had feared. Just a few days in, our next-door neighbor Victor had this epiphany that he had something in common with his Protestant friends. Victor's mother was from Mexico and his father from the Caribbean; they were a Catholic family. Victor discovered that the Bible his parents had on their coffee table held the same stories that we had been talking about and decided to bring his Bible to Backyard Bible Club.

Victor was Clayton's first and truest friend, and Ben regularly supervised them both. Solidarity had been born earlier that summer when they dug a really nice hole in the vacant lot next to our homes. Now discovering that we shared the same spiritual story was like magic to the kids. Victor hauled his family Bible across the street, and it was clear he had a burning desire for someone to affirm that he was truly part of the stories that were unfolding in our backyard. My friend and pastor, Mike, who looked like Kevin Costner or Harrison Ford, was there, and for some reason Victor, who was three-feet-nothing, looked up to him with awe and admiration. Victor just needed Mike to confirm what Victor and the boys already knew: Victor was a part of the club. So Victor drops his big Bible in Mike's lap and simply asks, "You like my Bible, Mike?" Mike examined his Bible slowly and methodically. You could tell he wanted to give Victor, who was probably five at the time, an honest assessment. Victor demanded no less. So after a few moments, Mike looked at Victor and said, "Your Bible is nice, but Victor, there's only one thing wrong with it." Victor looked utterly crushed. Mike then touched Victor's face. "Victor," Mike went on, "in your Bible, these pictures of Jesus look way too much like me. Truth is, Victor, Jesus looked way more like you!" Victor started to laugh. Not only did he share the same story, but the most important character had a family resemblance with Victor's family, not Ben and Clayton's. Jesus wasn't brought to our neighborhood by the family hosting Backyard Bible Club. Jesus was already there, and he looked a lot like our buddy Victor.

If we are going to be Christians who love the world and are willing to get close enough to feel, see, and hear it, we have to embrace the unfamiliar, the unknown, and the uncomfortable. The beauty of the unfamiliar is the beauty I found in a big construction worker, the vulnerability of reaching out to a group of parents living out a different faith tradition than mine, and the joy in the eyes of a little boy who discovered God looked a lot like him. For me this kind of encounter has happened mostly in cities, where I am constantly met with difference. If we can refuse the impulse to run back to what is familiar and comfortable, cities and other places of diversity can tell us the best and the worst about ourselves, and a little about doing justice in the world. My encouragement to all of us is to get close to difference, find places and people that are different than you, and then, rather than simply being frustrated with those differences, hang around long enough, suspending your own opinion to give yourself space to become somewhat fascinated with difference.

CHAPTER 2

LAMENT

Bitterly she weeps at night, tears are on her cheeks. Among all her lovers there is no one to comfort her. All her friends have betrayed her; they have become her enemies. Her filthiness clung to her skirts; she did not consider her future. Her fall was astounding; there was none to comfort her. "Look, LORD, on my affliction, for the enemy has triumphed."

— LAMENTATIONS 1:2, 9

For my new position as the associate professor of theology and culture at The Seattle School of Theology and Psychology, I head downtown every morning by train around seven. This particular morning was no different than any other late October morning in Seattle. It was rainy, windy, and cold, a reminder that summer was truly over and November was on its way.

But this morning, as I emerged from the train tunnel, I saw a crazy old homeless man huddled in the corner, attempting to shield himself from the horizontal rain. You could smell the pungent stench

31

of perspiration and see that he was simultaneously chilled and feverish. He talked to no one in particular — in fact, it was unclear whether he needed a conversation partner at all. He was alone, except, of course, for the voices that accompanied him. Mental illness is truly horrible!

Thirty years earlier a fragile, mentally ill boy had walked into the New Horizons drop-in center for street youth. Within minutes, our staff had assessed the situation and knew what

///
I can't get close to those who suffer without coming to grips with my own inability to help, myself or others.
\\\

we needed to do. It was something we almost never did. We helped the other kids pack up their belongings, closed the drop-in center, locked the front door, and called the mental health professionals. We told them we had a very vulnerable kid who needed a mental health assessment and a referral to a safe place to stay. We sat with the skinny young boy for six hours until some folks came, evaluated the boy's mental health status, and took him into care. In this boy's case, there was no time for relationship building, no time to empower the young person to work toward a self-determined exit strategy from street life. This broken early adolescent would not survive on the street, and the situation called for immediate action. He needed to be protected from the street and the harm he might do to himself. Miraculously, the boy was in an adolescent mental health facility by dark. It was a proactive intervention that had immediate results — we had been helpful and he was safe.

That October morning, I walked past the man who, 30 years ago, had been that boy. I heard his voice, and it rang through me. I knew it instantly. Then I recognized the face hidden in the hoodie. That day I was confronted with the illusion I had comforted myself with — that my helping was enough. I was hit with the realization that maybe I couldn't really ever make things better. I interrogated myself, asking, "Have I ever really relieved the suffering of anyone?" This weathered, ill man reminded me of so many others. The world is still broken. Heroin addicts still die, young people are still sold for sex, kids are still shot in school, and fourteen-year-old mentally ill boys turn into crazy old men on the street. Can I really make any of it better?

As I walked to the graduate school, I felt waves of despair. I was reeling, and felt absolutely nauseous. Why was I so shocked by this man's suffering? What was in me that so needed this to be different, for it to have turned out better? Sure, a lot of it had to do with genuine care for this human being. No one deserves to struggle with their mental health to such a degree that they are forced to survive on the street. And I don't want to become jaded and dismiss loving the world as a ridiculous act that only foolish, disillusioned people do. But the questions I asked myself had to do with the degree of shock I felt at this reminder of continued suffering: Why did I so deeply believe that I should have been able to make this man's life better? Why do I feel the need to make every unjust situation I come across better? Am I just setting myself up for endless disappointment? Why am I so shocked when my helping doesn't help, and what do I do when I am reminded I cannot fix it all? These seem like crucial questions to ask as we talk about walking into the injustice of this world.

What do I do when I fight for a kid and, 30 years later, see him literally three blocks from where I left him? I realized

///
The despair was threatening to overpower me.
\\\

33

part of my disorientation came from a place of helplessness. I don't know what else to do when I have fought for the good and it seems to have made no difference. And at an even deeper level, I began to realize, the broken man huddled in the corner reminded me of the places in my own life that, even with diligent attention, still feel like a raw wound. I can't get close to someone else's suffering without coming face-to-face with my own brokenness. Maybe this is part of the reason why I hope and pray that the suffering in this world goes away. It reminds me of my own inability to fix myself. I can't get close to those who suffer without coming to grips with my own inability to help, myself or others, and the powerlessness that rises up inside me when I can't fix everything . . . or anything. What was all this I was feeling?

Canadian theologian Douglass John Hall, in his book *The Cross in Our Context: Jesus and the Suffering World*, has helped me name this struggle. He explains that our attempts to manage our own and others' suffering and feelings of powerlessness can lead to what he labels as covert despair. This covert despair, he argues, is the illness of North American Christianity.

As I walked away from the man I once knew, I felt the impact of this denial, and the implications of suffering denied. In particular, I felt the insufficiency of my theology to imagine a good God alongside the existence of such suffering. As I felt my own helplessness, I grasped for any coping mechanism, any emotional pacifier that would inoculate me from that

///

But when we honestly examine ourselves, we must acknowledge that all of us, in our own way, are guilty and innocent. All of us are both perpetrators and victims.

\\\

34

feeling of powerlessness. My
need to put pain away from
me was working overtime to
resist the despair. The despair
was threatening to overpower
me. I couldn't deny what I had
just seen, couldn't push it away
by helping someone else. No

The "you get what you deserve" theology is critically important for those who have a lot of resources and are then faced with the fact that others have very little.

drug could inoculate me from the feelings that boiled within me:
I had helped and it hadn't made a difference. But maybe there was
another way. And maybe it had something to do with simply admitting what I was feeling, and that the world is broken.

Sometimes it is easier to figure out how to help when we can
define clearly who is innocent and who is guilty, and make black-
and-white judgments about who deserves their plight. A well-
used method to deny suffering altogether is to blame or justify the
condition of the poor soul we come in contact with. But when we
honestly examine ourselves, we must acknowledge that all of us, in
our own way, are guilty and innocent. All of us are both perpetrators
and victims. And once we do that, how we manage the reality that
human beings suffer gets far more complicated.

As I read the Book of Job, I have grown to believe that this
short book is trying to correct the impulse in us that falls back on
simplistic categories of guilt versus innocence, deserving versus
undeserving. The Book of Job overturns the theology that good
people do well and bad people pay a price. The doctrine of Job's
friends is that you get what you deserve. To be frank, the "you get
what you deserve" theology is critically important for those who

have a lot of resources and are then faced with the fact that others have very little.

///
To be grateful for suffering is to be grateful for your humanity.
**

But Job claims over and over that he has been a right-eous man, yet he still suffers greatly. The implication is that good and righteous people suffer too. The innocent clearly suffer in this world. The innocent go hungry and the innocent die, and it's not right, and it's unfair, and it still happens. Job teaches us that suffering has nothing to do with karma or retribution or good and bad people. But we cling to these arguments because they help us rationalize and make sense of the very thing we are all so afraid of — suffering.

I would imagine you have never thought of comedian Stephen Colbert as a philosopher or a theologian. But in an article in *Rolling Stone* magazine, writer Martin Schoeller asked Colbert about the tragic loss of his father and brothers, and he responded in a surprising way:

> Not to get too deep here, but the most valuable thing I can think of is to be grateful for suffering. That is a sublime feeling and completely inexplicable and illogical, but no one doesn't suffer. So the degree to which you can be aware of your own humanity is to the degree to which you can accept, with open eyes, your own suffering. To be grateful for suffering is to be grateful for your humanity, because what else are we going to do — say, "No, thanks"?

I think Colbert is on to something here. We all hate to suffer.

Suffering exposes us to the vulnerable state of being human, and is a reminder of all we can't fix. It puts many of our theological categories into question, makes us feel psychologically vulnerable and physically fragile. But, what Colbert is saying is that the very nature of suffering and my inability to control it puts me in some sort of solidarity with the broken-down man, the boy in the corner of the bus tunnel. More often than not, another person's pain unveils all of my own — so I of course have an aversion to entering into it. It confronts the defense mechanism that I use to feel OK. This is why it is very tough to allow oneself to truly feel another's suffering. Our efficient, sure-fire solutions — the ones we can report to donors in annual reports — are often simply a form of avoidance. And when the solutions don't work, blaming the victim can become another type of avoidance.

///

I believe that we all really do want to do what's best. There are times when our helping strategies work. Well-trained and hardworking people collaborating to come up with creative solutions are solving complex global problems. But where I get stuck is in how we respond when we realize we can't make all the problems go away. When we can't make things better, we tend to avoid or deny the sense of powerlessness that comes with that realization. When we can't help, we are confronted with our own mortality, our own suffering, and our own inability to fix things — and this is terrifying. If we are not careful, we do all kinds of psychological gymnastics to avoid these feelings because we don't know how to manage them. And when we turn to helping others in order to cover our own pain, this helping can be a form of denial. It takes great courage to admit we don't always know what's best for others. Sometimes we can't help,

CHAPTER 2

and that feels horrible. In that feeling we confront the terrifying confession that this world is filled with suffering that we can't fix, and that we, too, are filled with pain that we can't make go away.

This was the source of the nausea I felt as I walked to school that October morning. I came face-to-face with a very personal form of suffering that I couldn't alleviate, and something in me was trying to avoid it. The most tragic thing is that as I ran from that feeling, I also ran away from the human being who sat huddled in the bus tunnel. Even if I had approached him, my own discomfort in that moment would not have been helpful

///
Solidarity makes us human.
It bears witness to how
out of control suffering
makes all of us feel.
**

for him. In my avoidance of his suffering, I avoided him, and I avoided the parts of me that intimately connected me to him — in Colbert's words, our common human suffering.

In all my years of going to church, I do not remember hearing a sermon on the biblical genre of poetry called lament. It seems to be avoided like, well, suffering. As someone who has spent his entire adult life studying Scripture, I have to ask myself why this type of poetry, so pervasive in Scripture, is often avoided or ignored in church. One-third of the Psalms are psalms of lament. Most of Job is a lament. And the entire Book of Lamentations is a classic lament. One of the last things Jesus cries out from the Cross before his death is a lament. He quotes Psalm 22: "My God, My God, why have you forsaken me?" What is the nature of lament, and why, if it is woven through so much Old Testament text, have I heard so little about it? The truth-telling of the lament is ancient poetry, told from the perspective of those who are suffering greatly, who have the freedom

38

to ask, along with the speaker in the Psalms: "God, where are You?" and "God, how could You?"

There is no section of Scripture more tragic, I would argue, than the Book of Lamentations. Kathleen M. O'Connor explores this much-avoided piece of biblical literature in *Lamentations and the Tears of the World*. The historical context of Lamentations is one of exile and abandonment. The leaders of Israel have been taken captive to Babylon. Jerusalem's political, religious, and economic leadership has been destroyed, and what is left is a struggling people without resources or hope. These weeping, directionless people are symbolically represented in Lamentations through the voice of Daughter Zion, who begs for someone to witness her pain. She cries out; she has been disregarded like a menstrual rag, tossed away, forgotten. She is left so desperate that she declares her only chance of survival is to eat her own young. There are multiple voices in Lamentations — the truth of this tragedy is told from multiple perspectives. But of crucial importance is the missing voice in Lamentations. The one voice that is not heard from is the voice of God. O'Connor argues that there is a good reason why God's voice is silent in the lament. You see, the voice of power almost always overshadows the voice of suffering, which comes from a place of weakness and total vulnerability. The voice of the suffering victim needs room to be heard — the voice of the Almighty would drown her out.[1]

As I think about all the suffering in the world, I am struck by this missing

///

Lament is the place where we as humans can declare our intense felt absence of God and the suffering that is part of how we experience our humanity in light of that absence.

**

39

voice. God does not speak, and in not speaking, allows His suffering Daughter Zion to say all that she needs to say. God is silent, and accusations about God are free to move from the subconscious and unspoken to loud declarations without filters. Daughter Zion's pain is not constricted by concerns for proper religious protocol. She can speak her truth about suffering, about how badly it hurts and how confusing it is. O'Connor goes on to say that this form of truth-telling in Scripture exposes wounds, gives voice to pain, and reverses denial and amnesia.

I find that lament is the place where we as humans can declare our intense felt absence of God and the suffering that is part of how we experience our humanity in light of that absence. Good people suffer, and sometimes we can do nothing. We can do nothing except be human with those who suffer. This form of solidarity denies denial. But it also demands that power be silent for the sake of those who need to say the unspeakable.

This solidarity makes us human. It bears witness to how out of control suffering makes all of us feel. The prayers of lament — "God how could You?" and "God, why can't You?"— bring us into alignment with the most broken places in the world.

Most of us have also had experiences of God as a healer and deliverer. And we might feel more comfortable proclaiming that God in the world. But all of us have also experienced places where we did not see God, those dark, terrifying places in our own soul and around the world. What do we do when we can't fix it and we can't fake it? I believe Scripture is pretty clear about this. Job suffered unjustly and so do a lot of others. There are times that God shows up in miraculous ways. But when God seems a long way off, we get the — dare I say — opportunity to enter into shared helplessness with those we hope to help. We can choose to deny denial. This is the gift that Colbert claims we can't say, "No, thanks" to — because to do so is to reject being human. And as much as none of us want to invite suffering into our lives, the truth is it might be — and probably is — already there. We can deny it, we can project onto others. But the invitation suffering brings us is simple, confusing, and so human: Will you enter into it and run the risk of being as powerless as those you so desperately want to help? Will you take the time to feel all that you need to feel, to pray a prayer of lament? Are you willing to accept those places where God says nothing and makes room for the voice of pain to say all that it needs to say?

Sometimes, as we walk with people, silence is the best gift we give. To be quiet and in solidarity, to say nothing, to make room for lament as we share in the forsakenness felt by a confused and abandoned humanity. Sometimes justice looks like simply allowing the voices of those who have been broken by the world to scream without filter, without restriction. Sometimes the most helpful thing to do is to cry and ask God, "How long, oh Lord, how long?"

HOW LONG, OH LORD, HOW LONG?

With a cup of coffee, I looked out my window and cried. I was looking across the street at the little house that was home to a sweet family and the dearest childhood friend my sons ever had — Victor. Victor was home on leave from the Marine Corps, in love with his new wife and celebrating his twenty-second birthday, when he was shot in his mother's driveway. His mother and father now both lived a few miles from us, but Victor would always stop by for my sons' birthdays or an occasional summer barbecue. We had known him his entire life.

Victor always seemed to rise above the toughness that can be associated with our neighborhood. His radiant smile and infectious, loud laugh were contagious. Even today, the sound of it rings in my head and makes me smile. He was happy to see you, always.

It's hard to remember my first memory of him. He was always with his older sister Maria in our front yard, from the time his family moved in across the street. At four he wore big black shorts and a red tank top, and had the best mullet of any four-year-old I have ever met. He came to our home one day wearing his underpants outside his jeans — it was OK, they were Batman underwear. His father, Mario, owned the corner store, and my boys grew up there, the store as their playground and Victor their constant playmate. And, as I mentioned in the last chapter, he brought the biggest Bible I have ever seen to Backyard Bible Club, his skinny arms wrapped around the big, white coffee table book filled with Rembrandt-type pictures of a fair-skinned Jesus. I will never forget the joy in Victor's laugh when Mike told him about the problem with his Bible's pictures of fair-skinned Jesus. Victor embraced the divine revelation that Jesus looked a lot more like him than the family that hosted Bible club. He reminded me of this revelation often.

We celebrated Victor's fifth birthday with his family at that house across the street. Victor must have run through our door five times that day, confirming that we were going to attend. We showed up on time and realized we were about two hours too early. It might have been the first meal we ate at a neighbor's home in Rainier Valley.

The last time I talked to Victor, I was walking out of Half Price Books. He was sitting in the adjacent storefront, the Marine recruiting station, and of course when he saw me, he yelled my name and ran across the parking lot to greet me. We hugged and laughed as I reminded him of one of our inside jokes.

Last summer, I looked over my own son's shoulder into the face of Victor, who was lying in a casket, grieving a Marine who didn't die in Afghanistan but in his mother's driveway on his twenty-second birthday from a stray bullet that penetrated his chest as he sat next to his new wife. I listened to the weeping of a mother who had lost her son and felt the cold shock of a father who wouldn't leave the side of a casket.

Out my living room window, the home across the street will be a constant reminder. He is gone. I couldn't protect him, couldn't save him. I couldn't save or protect any of them. The days following the funeral, I felt absolutely powerless. Deserted. All I can do is ask, with my sons and wife, my neighbors, and with my community:

> *How long, LORD? Will you forget me forever? How long will you hide your face from me? How long must I wrestle with my thoughts and day after day have sorrow in my heart? How long will my enemy triumph over me? Look on me and answer, LORD my God.*
>
> — PSALM 13:1–3

I couldn't begin to imagine what Victor's father felt as he stood next to his son's body. I know I felt only a tiny fraction of what the family was experiencing—in fact, it feels unfair to make any comparison at all. I will never know their devastation. But as I write this, my own grief wells up in my throat, and I find myself pushing it back down, trying to keep it at bay. So, my lament is in this small solidarity with others who cry. I understand better what it is like to feel forsaken by the presence of the God I have so often preached about. I never asked for or sought out this kind of solidarity with another human being. I cringe at the words often attributed to the martyred bishop Oscar Romero: "There are many things that can only be seen through eyes that have cried." So, sometimes I just cry:

> *My God, my God, why have you forsaken me? Why are you so far from saving me, so far from my cries of anguish? My God, I cry out by day, but you do not answer, by night, but I find no rest.*
>
> — PSALM 22:1–2

In the crucifixion narratives, Jesus is quoting Psalm 22, this tragic cry of abandoned, bewildered humanity. "My God, my God why have you forsaken me?" This is the moment that I would argue most identifies Jesus with all of us in our humanity. It is in His death that Jesus prays this prayer of self-emptying. God is absent, gone in this moment. In this death, there is a space created in the life of Jesus that feels tragic and terrifying. But in this moment of God's absence, of Jesus dying and experiencing the loneliness of a human being encountering death, of being forsaken by God, He lets the most tragic part of being human into Himself. In this act, Jesus welcomes the forsakenness of humanity into Himself. In this God-forsaken moment of God dying, the divine makes room for all that is human — even death and despair — welcoming it all into God's self. It is in this empty, lonely place of isolation and despair that allows for God's absence to paradoxically make room for God himself. Jesus on the

Cross doesn't quote all of Psalm 22, only the part that tells the world He has embraced the forsakenness of humanity.

To me, this lament is God's most hospitable act, letting the most tragic part of the human condition into Himself. The fear of being forsaken, the shame that we might deserve to be forsaken, and the declaration that we are alone. The Almighty makes space, welcoming every part of us in.

Lament is not passive acceptance or resignation. Lament actively declares the way things are, without consent or justification. Lament is testimony that demands the victims and sufferers in this world be given the right to speak for themselves. Courageously declaring what is wrong in the world, lament creates an empty, lonely space for what is right, for what is supposed to be. For the world's sake, are we willing to get close enough to be honest about our feelings of shared helplessness, to raise our voices in lament? If the prayer of Jesus makes room in God for human forsakenness, maybe in our declaration of God's absence, we too can makes space for God's self to be revealed in us.

SETTING A DIFFERENT TABLE, CREATING SPACE FOR THE OTHER

I have never really liked to fly, and when my sons were young, it became a paralyzing anxiety, for multiple reasons. You can get the whole story from my therapist. Simply put, my dad died when I was three, and when my own sons were young children — who loved and worshiped *their* dad — I began to realize once again the hole that had opened up in me when I lost my father. The plane became a symbol of both my lack of control and the fear that my boys would experience the loss that I had endured, the loss that still had a hold of me. Every time I boarded a plane, I would envision myself being taken away from them. It was terrifying. Through much prayer, some good therapeutic interactions, and a supportive community, I would fly and at times feel OK. I could manage. But at other times, fear would raise its ugly head, and I felt like a dead man walking. I was heading to the gallows. I just knew that the plane would crash and my boys would have to negotiate the world alone like I did. I kept talking and praying and trying to move forward. But fear was my closest travel companion.

Then, about 12 years ago, upon the invitation of a graduate school providing a class in India, I reluctantly boarded a plane to Mumbai, the second international trip of my life. (I choose not to count trips to Canada. Sorry,

///
It really didn't even feel like love. It was simply giving my friend the benefit of the doubt rather than letting my terror push me to ridiculous conclusions.
**

Canada.) This was soon after the tragedy of 9/11, and I wasn't the only one who felt some level of fear about flying. The fact that I knew others shared some of my panic was a strange comfort to me.

I realized even then that, in some ways, my fear feels good to me, like it might be the only thing that saves me. Fear, I would remind myself, is sometimes a legitimate warning sign of danger. Why would I let go of the warning mechanism that might preserve my life and get me back to Linda, Ben, and Clayton? As I found my seat on the plane to Mumbai, I began a "Coach Ron" conversation with myself — the one where I tell myself that I am doing "God's work," so of course I will be fine. This is rather ridiculous, I realize, when I stop to think of how many people have done "God's work" and didn't end up fine. Hebrews 11 has a whole list of men and women who followed the path of faith; some experienced the promise of the Messiah, and others were sawed in two.

As I tried to calm myself with faulty platitudes, a gentleman pointed to the seat next to me. I was in the aisle seat. I love those aisle seats. I can manage my whole row. Never an exit row, though. I have no desire to be responsible for leading anyone else in my row to safety as we all fall out of the sky from 30,000 feet. But the aisle — ah, yes! That I can handle. And by "handle," I mean to give people the OK, as they feel the need, to climb over me to use the washroom, and to take the responsibility of distributing in-flight snacks. The glorious aisle seat gives me the freedom to get up any time I want and drop my own garbage in the bag coming down the aisle. All the control with little real responsibility.

As my new friend worked his way into the middle seat, I went about my inventory — everything in its proper place, headphones, snacks, water, pillow. Then I was interrupted by a thought that suddenly dropped into my head from nowhere. The man who had just sat down next to me. Didn't he look . . . Middle Eastern? I am not proud of the intrapersonal conversation that began to bounce around in my head, but I feel obligated to own it. "He looks Middle Eastern?" I questioned myself. "Ron Ruthruff, what is that supposed to mean? He's a thirty-five-year-old man taking the same plane to the same place you're going!" "But what if he's — " I said to myself in as rational a tone as possible — "you know, a *bad guy*?" "What do you mean a bad guy?" "You know. A terrorist." These thoughts ping-ponged against my skull. I felt like I couldn't slow them down, let alone stop them. So then I start to berate myself: "Ron Ruthruff, you should be ashamed of yourself!" "I know and I'm sorry! But if he is a terrorist, what do I do?" At this point the voice of panic and control took over. It sounded a lot like the principal of my junior high, firm and correct. "If you get up and simply mention — calmly — the word *terrorist* to the flight attendant . . . Fear was overpowering me. I could recognize that

///

If I was wrong and, by some slim chance, love killed me when fear would have let me live, then — I decided this all of a sudden in that moment — dying didn't seem that bad.

**

the fear was ridiculous, but what if it was right? Taking the slightest chance that I was right could save my life. If I was wrong, I would be embarrassed, but I would live to be an embarrassment to my boys.

Then a voice much deeper than my fear spoke. "What if you love?" it asked. "What if you give him the very same benefit of the doubt he is giving you? What if this time you don't wager on fear but on love?" "OK, Ron. Fair enough. But what if you love, and you're *wrong and you die*?" In this brief moment, I made a decision that was, quite honestly, life-changing. I decided to love. Fear seemed the safer bet. Fear would insulate and protect me. Love was not safe at all. It felt like total vulnerability. Love felt like I was jumping from that plane without a parachute. But quietly, within myself, I thought, "I think I would rather love." It really didn't even feel like love. It was simply giving my friend the benefit of the doubt rather than letting my terror push me to ridiculous conclusions. All I really created was space—space for a man I did not know, for him to live beyond my fear and my stereotypes. If I was wrong and, by some slim chance, love killed me when fear would have let me live, then—I decided this all of a sudden in that moment—dying didn't seem that bad. Living in the middle of fear seemed no longer to be an option. So I sat back, took a breath, and silently accepted what would happen next.

I leaned over and introduced myself. We talked briefly, and then both figured out how we were going to survive a 12-hour flight sharing the same armrest. I never found out his religious persuasion, or where he was from. And, obviously, I didn't die. But something in me did die a little that day. I died to something that I was relying on to keep my life afloat that *needed* to pass away, and learned that it made some space in me for others—even those who I thought were my enemies — and that space felt roomy and good. What I thought would open me up to danger opened me up to discovering something new, for some*one* new, beyond my assumptions.

///

I have always been intrigued by the home of Mary and Martha that Jesus is invited to in Luke 10. So many times in Luke's story, when the people who seem to be furthest from the kingdom of God invite Jesus over, they all have a great time. But when Jesus eats with those who have political power or religious clout, it ends up like one of those holiday dinners where things get awkward too quickly for anyone to enjoy the meal. In this story, Luke calls this house the *house of Mary and Martha.* Imagine, in the first century, referring to a house as belonging to the two women rather than their brother Lazarus. I wonder what Luke is trying to tell us. For now, I want to focus on Mary and Martha and how I believe that they both chose to offer hospitality — to make space for the other — but in radically different ways.

Martha appears to be the good host. She does what we all do — gets busy preparing a meal for the guests. Mary ends up not helping with dinner prep, but rather sits with Jesus, listening to His every word. This upsets Martha. She is frustrated that her sister isn't being a good host and complains to Jesus. Jesus simply tells her that Mary has made the better choice. Many have claimed that in this, Jesus differentiates between choosing to do and choosing to be. Mary chooses rightly, and it won't be taken from her. I actually think this tells us far more about different ways to be hospitable as we welcome others into our space and life.

Martha does exactly what I am inclined to do in the name of hospitality. I love inviting people into my home. I love to barbecue, and

/ / /

These moments when we are truly present for the sake of mutual transformation are time altering.

\\\

rumor has it that the love that I put into it results in pretty delicious food. When people come over to our house, they have a good meal and usually a good time, and there is absolutely nothing wrong with that. Hospitality can be about a host setting a good table for his guests. But when I think about this type of hospitality and evaluate what's happening, I realize that I am usually the one choosing the menu and making the rules. I am, for the most part, in control. Like Martha, I am doing and creating, and my guest, if he or she is a good guest, takes cultural cues from me as the host and simply plays by my rules. But Mary has a different way of hosting. She sits, she listens, and in some way, she turns the table and allows Jesus, the guest, to lead. Jesus is now the teacher, and Mary has created space in her home for Him to be who He is. It is almost like they have switched places. In listening, she opens herself up to her guest's agenda. The guest now has the opportunity to occupy a space that was once occupied by the host.

Henri J. M. Nouwen explores this idea of hospitality in his book *Reaching Out: The Three Movements of the Spiritual Life*, calling for a disarming way of hosting that he contrasts with a kind of hostility that he believes underlies much of what is done in the name of hospitality. This hostility, as he refers to it, is exemplified in fearful efforts to manage and control our guest — perhaps, I would guess, because we are concerned with feeling good about ourselves and protecting our self-image by achieving the status of the perfect host. I am so familiar with this impulse to invite a guest and make sure all is perfect, and I am convicted that much of this is tied to my desire to project an image that is complete, in need of nothing from my guest except compliance. Nouwen presents a beautifully rich definition of hospitality in which the host lets go for the sake of the guest: "The paradox of hospitality is that it wants to create emptiness, not a fearful emptiness, but a friendly emptiness where strangers discover themselves." As I read Nouwen's radical rethinking of hospitality, I thought about the many times that as a guest I felt the awkward sense of not knowing the rules. I thought of my seat partner on that plane and how fear — my fear — created so many preconceived notions that there was no room for me to discover him. I had filled that space with my conclusions, making me feel like I could manage our interaction with no, or at least little, risk to myself. Once I entertained a different posture, a posture of openness and love, it definitely felt like entering into a risky space, a space where he himself, and not my ideas about him, could be present.

This Nouwen way of being hospitable is exemplified in Mary sitting at the feet of Jesus. It is not about control but about cultivating a holy emptiness for the sake of those who sit with us. This emptiness is one that allows room for guests to be released from our agenda and to discover and define their true selves. But this also means our guest is free to discover themselves in their own time and in their own way. Therefore, as I host, I must suspend my own judgment and agenda and trust the Spirit to manage the space between me and my

///

Living in this moment with another person, holding the past and the future at bay for the sake of now, is eternal, the present now of eternity.

**

guests. All of a sudden, power and control seem to switch hands.[1]

These types of interactions move from transaction to mutual transformation. We stop using conversation to make the other person a lot more like us. We stop listening for the sole reason of devising ways to change the other person's mind. These moments when we are truly present for the sake of mutual transformation are time altering. For me, to be totally present with another person stops time. The past (where I have been, how I have failed) and the future (what I hope to accomplish) are both disregarded for the eternal *now*. Living in this moment with another person, holding the past and the future at bay for the sake of now, is eternal, the present now of eternity. This sort of hospitality honors the image of God in the guest. It is Mary suspending what Martha thought was necessary to be with the other in eternity.

It is letting go of fear and control for the sake of allowing space where we get the opportunity to truly hear each other and be human together — and those interactions can be magical.

A PLACE FOR LOITERERS AND TRESPASSERS

I once worked with a street chaplain who was a little eccentric. In one of our conversations, he told me that he wanted to start doing communion on the street, inviting whomever he could find to share in the Lord's Supper. He invited me to go with him, and on a rainy, cold night in February we headed out. I have always said that a 37-degree rainy February night in Seattle is much colder than a 25-degrees-below-zero day in Fairbanks, Alaska. That night was proof that my theory was correct. It was windy and cold. We walked around a street called Broadway, the main drag in Capitol Hill, home to one of the city's community colleges and to volumes of students, home-less folks, poor people, and kids on the street. Lee, the chaplain, had done it up right.

///
Mercy and justice invites all
of us to a table.
**

No little wafers and shot glasses of grape juice for this communion. Lee brought a huge cooler on rollers. It was filled with bread, fruit juice, and hot cocoa. Lee had slathered the bread with olive oil and great spices. It smelled amazing. I was getting excited about sharing a rainy night communion with anyone who showed up.

We walked around the streets, and Lee simply invited folks who seemed to be hanging out to join us. They all knew Lee, and knew he was clergy. His invitation was accepted by a few. Earlier in the year, Lee had gathered together some of the homeless young people he knew to participate in a similar communion adventure at Golden Gardens Park, on Puget Sound. He had drawn a connection between the ocean setting and stories about Jesus teaching by the lake or the sea. I guess many of the folks we met that night already knew Lee's invitations were always creative.

We began to walk down Broadway. A few kids from the street, a couple of college kids, and an older homeless man who appeared to need to get something into his stomach had joined us. By this time it was raining pretty hard. Sheets of water were blowing in sideways, and we knew we had to find shelter. It's pretty hard to ask a restaurant for a table for six when you've brought your own food, so that wasn't an option. The park nearby, with its dripping tree branches and soggy grass, wasn't an appealing option either. So we looked for an alcove or building awning to give us some temporary shelter. We ended up at the community college.

It was late, classes were out, and the campus was dark. We went around the back and found what looked to be a perfect spot. It was an

///
Love prompted me to make room for the complex identity of the man next to me.
**

entrance set into the wall, three feet wide, dry, and shielded from the wind. Lee got out the elements, along with big cups and napkins, and began to pass around the meal. Lee's words were simple: "You are invited to share a meal with Jesus, and as we share this meal together, we act out the story of Jesus until we can eat it with Him."

I don't know what distracted me, but my eye caught a sign — weathered but readable — on the alcove wall. *No trespassing, loitering, or illegal activity permitted.* "Where is illegal activity permitted?" I smirked to myself. Then I began to digest the significance of the situation. The message Lee shared with us as we ate together was that we all belonged. I thought of the meal Jesus shared with His disciples, described in Luke 22:14–16, where He expresses His longing for all of us to one day break bread together:

> *And when the hour came, [Jesus] reclined at table, and the apostles with Him. And He said to them, I have earnestly and intensely desired to eat this Passover with you before I suffer; For I say to you, I shall eat it no more until it is fulfilled in the kingdom of God.* (AMP)

Wait a second. As we sat in that alcove, I was beginning to experience a table set for all of us. Mercy and justice invites all of us to a table. We sat and began to see a table emerge, in a space that was not for us — that was clear. But what also became clear was that the meal was showing us — reminding us — that there *is* a place where no one is accused of loitering, where no one is trespassing, and where those who think they are excluded are told they belong. This is the story of God setting a bigger table for all of us.

As I think back to that plane ride so long ago, it was really about me creating space. That early morning on the way to Mumbai, fear was in control of my space. To relinquish it felt absolutely dangerous. But, in the end, love prompted me to make room for the complex identity of the man next to me, an identity that was much more expansive than the image my fear had projected onto him.

Are we willing to set a bigger table? How willing are we to simply create space? Are we willing to sit at tables where we create space for others? Space that suspends judgment and conclusions long enough for others to discover where they fit in the story of God.

Here's what I do know: the table is set in places we can't imagine, with guests we might not invite. At this table, Jesus is host, enemies are friends, and we are all guests. This is the place where we get to bear witness to the gulf between the kingdom of our God and the kingdom of this world.

CHAPTER 4

FINDING WHERE THE KINGDOM GROWS

A while back I was reading a lectionary text and was struck by Jesus' words: "Follow me." A few days later, one of my clergy friends from Street Psalms, who enjoys deep reflection on these sorts of ideas, sent me the Street Psalms monthly newsletter that included an article he had written, titled "Meal From Below," on this idea of following Jesus. (Street Psalms is a group of Christ-centered people who are passionate about cultivating communities of grassroots leaders among those who have been labeled the least, last, and lost in our world.)

My friend presented the idea that the Eucharist (the Lord's Supper) is a mobile table. Jesus is the host, and we're always the guests. The table doesn't sit in one place. The implication of this idea is that our spiritual journey of discernment is to detect where the table *is* and where the table *is not*. I was intrigued by the connection between a movable table, the invitation of Jesus to follow Him, and the idea that our task is to discover where He's hosting a table for us.

The article encouraged us to walk—literally. To really take a walk, follow Jesus, and discover the table. So I decided to do it. I hoped that somehow, as I headed downtown, I would find out where I needed to go even though, practically speaking, I didn't need directions.

So I got on the train downtown and tried to follow Jesus. It was about ten a.m., and the train was almost empty. A couple of passen-

///
"Don't look at him," I said to myself. "He'll know you have a dollar."
\\\

gers sat in front, and I found my way to the very back. I love sitting in the back, whether it's on the train or in a café. I want to see everything that's going on around me. I'm like the gambler in the old westerns who sits in the saloon with his chair leaning up against the wall. Mostly though, I just like to be in control. As I realized this, I laughed. Following Jesus might be tougher than I thought.

At the next stop down the line, a group of young men got on. They walked to the back where I was sitting and plopped down around me. *They must like control, too,* I thought. They were typical teenagers wearing stereotypical urban gear: great tennis shoes, flat-brimmed baseball hats, and neatly pressed jeans. It's humbling and frustrating that, even after 25 years living in Rainier Valley, a racially diverse neighborhood in Seattle, when a group of young people from a different ethnic group than I am gets on the train, I pay extra attention. Would I have felt the same way if it had been a bunch of white kids? It's more than frustrating—it's tragic that the messages I've absorbed from the dominant culture still shape my notion of what these young African-American men bring with them when they step on the train. We rode on.

As we traveled downtown, I just couldn't spot Jesus. I tried listening to Rage Against the Machine on my iPod. Nope, no Jesus. I started reading my Bible. Jesus is all over the pages, but today He wasn't there. And I was reading the Gospel of Luke; I always find Jesus in Luke!

A few more stops went by and a white man got on the train. He was a little drunk and perhaps developmentally disabled. He was filthy, too, maybe homeless. He was tattooed, but they weren't really good tattoos. They were the kind of tattoos you get at a party when you're seventeen years old, or in prison. He had a homemade tattoo on his forehead. It was a pentagram. I didn't know exactly what this meant, but to a boy raised Pentecostal, it looked like Satan to me.

He was a pathetic-looking soul. He mumbled something unintelligible to the guys with the great shoes and perfect ball caps. He asked again, and then a third time. We all got it the third time. "Can I have some change to catch the bus to Tacoma?" I immediately averted my eyes. "Don't look at him," I said to myself. "He'll know you have a dollar." Yikes! I hate this kind of moment. It's awkward and uncomfortable. A few worlds were colliding on the back of the train, and there I was, trying my best to avoid them all.

The guys in the cool shoes looked at the dirty, tattooed drunk, and then at each other. Then, in this moment of spontaneous spiritual impulse, they said nothing, but simply began to pool their change. One guy looked at the tattooed, filthy man and asked, "Why do you have a satanic tattoo on your forehead?" *Great question,* I thought to myself. The drunk guy spoke innocently: "I'm not a Satanist. I'm a Christian." Another guy corrected his friend, "Don't you know that man looks on the outside, but God looks on the heart?" The young man's words floored me. I'd completely misjudged this situation.

By this time the offering had been collected, and there was almost enough for bus fare. It was only then I gave my dollar out of guilt, knowing that, in this moment on the train, I had seen Jesus. He asked me to follow, and I had to participate in the offering, late and ashamed.

I came out of the train tunnel and hopped on a bus. The tattooed man wasn't too far behind, headed to a smoke shop to get his bus ticket or, more likely, a pack of smokes. The table was gone as quickly as it had appeared.

Maybe this is where spiritual formation gets real — how it takes on flesh: when we look for Jesus in the faces of those who carry on their backs all the preconceived ideas and brokenness of our communities. Maybe following Jesus means to keep looking and keep walking — even in places that feel like chaos — training our ears and eyes to see Him. We knock and seek and ask, and Jesus reveals himself. In this moment, we take the bread and wine and eat it. Then it's gone.

Like the manna of the Old Testament, it's given to us, but we can't hold on to it or store it. If we do, it spoils.

Or maybe, like the mustard seed in Jesus' parable, the kingdom grows when and where it wants, and it's on us to take notice. So we walk on, trying to listen and to see. Knowing that Jesus will reveal Himself again on some other train, at some other time.

SEEDS OF THE KINGDOM

I love the story of Jesus told in the Gospel of Mark. It's a fast-paced, action-packed short story that teaches us the way of discipleship, the way of following Jesus. And it does so not in the manner we expect. Over and over we learn who Jesus is and how to follow Him through the disciples' negative examples and hardheaded blunders. For me, this has always been of great comfort. It's humbling to admit this, but I'm just like the disciples, who in the beginning follow Jesus thinking they have it all figured out, then run headlong into situations where they need Jesus to reveal Himself through the most unlikely characters and in the strangest of places.

To me, the fact that even Jesus' closest friends needed help understanding what He was saying and doing suggests we might be best off taking a humble posture as Jesus invites us to follow Him and love the world.

WHAT THE KINGDOM LOOKS LIKE: WHERE IT GROWS AND WHO GETS IT

In Mark 4:1–33, Jesus tells three parables about seed and soil. He wanted to describe what the kingdom of God looks like, who can understand it, and where it will grow.

In these stories, Jesus conjures some evocative images. In the parable of the sower, a farmer goes out to plant his field and, according to each type of soil and its growing conditions, some of the seeds grow and some die. In the parable of the growing seed, another farmer plants, and while he sleeps, the seed miraculously grows. And in the parable of the mustard seed, the kingdom is likened to a small mustard seed that grows into a large plant.

Let's start with the parable of the mustard seed. It's the story of how something seemingly insignificant grows into something big. The mustard plant is really not a plant at all but an uncontrollable and pesky weed that was considered unclean to the Jewish culture.

Even though the seed is tiny, with a little help it's able to grow aggressively and become a huge shrub. But the metaphor is not just about size. It's also about the *type* of plant that Jesus chose. Why didn't He pick a seed that produces something impressive, like a tree or plant of epic and stately proportion? If I were to choose a tree that exemplifies my idea of the kingdom of God, I'd pick a cedar, or the magnificent, evergreen Douglas fir. But Jesus wanted the mustard plant. It's like choosing a dandelion as the emblem for the kingdom of God — the weeds that I spend hours each summer trying to remove from my lawn. This is not what I expect the kingdom to look like.

///
But Jesus wanted the mustard plant. It's like choosing a dandelion as the emblem for the kingdom of God.
\\\

When I think about that day I took the train downtown, I'm reminded of the pesky mustard seed. When I got onto the train, I discovered a table — or maybe a kingdom — growing in a place and among people I didn't expect.[1]

In the parable of the growing seed, a farmer plants seeds, and while he sleeps, they sprout, mature, and grow. He doesn't control the process, and has no idea why or how the growth happened.

Years ago, when I worked with homeless youth in Seattle through a ministry called New Horizons, we were intentional about marking the significant life events in the lives of these teens. Birthdays were a big deal. Celebrating birthdays tangibly communicated, "I'm glad you were born!" This was a huge gift for kids who, through all the pain of family dysfunction and street life, often wondered why they were born or why they were alive. We were also intentional about celebrating other successes, like when a young person successfully got their state ID, passed the GED, or graduated from treatment.

On one such occasion, we gathered for a housewarming party. Tabitha, a young woman, had just graduated from drug treatment and moved into a new apartment. So what do you do when someone gets her first apartment? You throw her a housewarming party and come loaded with gifts.

One of the staff had gone to Costco and set out treats on the small kitchen table. Most of us sat on the avocado green carpet, a holdover from 1976. Tabitha sat in the room's only chair. Looking up at her, I remember thinking to myself, "Wow, kids just seem to glow after 90 days in a health treatment facility." And glow she did. Her hair shone, her eyes sparkled, and the tattoo colors inked into her skin looked deep and rich.

Tabitha began to open her presents. There were dish towels, and a toaster oven to complement the apartment's stove top. The gifts were really not that special, but as she opened each one, Tabitha let out a shriek of joy.

"No way! You've gotta be kidding me!"

Finally, I just had to ask in the middle of her exclamations, "Tabitha, why are you so excited? The gifts really aren't that great."

"No!" she said emphatically. "The gifts are great, but that's not what blows me away." Now she had everyone's attention.

We all leaned in as if to ask in unison: "Then what?"

Tabitha laughed at what was so clear to her that the rest of us were missing. "It's all of you," she said. "It's all of you in my apartment!"

We obviously looked like we still needed more explanation. Tabitha laughed again. "It's that all my best friends are Christians!"

In that moment I discovered something. It was the kingdom of God. To my surprise, and in ways I couldn't begin to explain, it was growing. Tabitha was not just a recipient of some housewarming gifts. She was a participating member in a community she never imagined herself being a part of. She was not being treated as a "client," but rather as an equal and a friend, and the boundary-breaking work was hilarious to her.

The kingdom was expanding before my eyes and it was beautiful. It was treating Tabitha with a gentle human touch and expanding into a shape I couldn't have imagined, in a place I wasn't expecting. But there it was. Growing around all of us who sat in a circle on avocado shag carpet.

The parable of the growing seed paints the picture of a kingdom that grows at night while the farmer sleeps. The parable of the mustard seed tells the story of a seed that looks insignificant yet shoots up like a weed when and where it wants. The kingdom is always a surprise, and we are not in control of how it takes root and thrives.

As Christians, we often use the parable of the scattered seed to support our impulse to dismiss folks who disagree with us. We refer to them as rocky soil, those unable to accept the Word. But this interpretation doesn't take into account the other two parables. One a story of seed that sprouts while the farmer sleeps — outside of his efforts and control — and the other a story of a tiny seed that grows bigger than anyone would have expected or thought possible.

Both parables challenge the common interpretation of the parable of the scattered seed. Growing up, I was told that the purpose of the church and a worthy disciple of Jesus was to find good soil and then plant the kingdom of God there. But I don't think that's what the story means. These other two parables aren't at all about carefully sifting soil to make sure it is good, and then planting seeds. Taken together, the three stories don't reflect a system in which Christians set up dogmas to find the exact right place to bring the kingdom into being. What Jesus seems to be offering is an invitation to enter into a mystery, one in which the kingdom springs up in ways we could never have imagined.

///

Jesus charged them to develop an attitude of openness to and awareness of what the kingdom of God was really about.

\\\

Jesus believed the disciples needed additional instruction in order to understand where the kingdom could be found, how it grew, and what hindered it from growing. He told them that if they didn't understand these things (Mark 4:13), it would be impossible to understand anything else. He knew that their misinformed expectations of what the kingdom should look like was interfering with their ability to identify the real thing — not only *where* the seed was growing, but also *what* the kingdom would look like once it was fully grown.

Jesus was teaching about cultivation, but the disciples didn't understand who or what needed to be cultivated. The answer was right in front of them — and obvious answers are sometimes the most difficult to recognize. He was talking about the soil of their own hearts, trying to help them understand that *they* were the ones who needed tilling, weeding, and nurturing in order to see and hear differently. He was showing them the necessity of tending to their hearts — and us tending to ours — so that they might be receptive to what the kingdom actually is, apart from their expectations of what it should be. Jesus charged them to develop an attitude of openness to and awareness of what the kingdom of God was really about.

It's true that in the parable of the scattered seed, the weeds, thistles, and hard ground make it difficult for the seed to grow. But rather than imagining ourselves as the farmers in the story, let's imagine ourselves as the soil. The weeds, thistles, and hard ground are the environmental factors that make it difficult for the seed to prosper: suffering, persecution, short attention spans, the desire for comfort, and a need to define the kingdom on our terms are all things that cloud our ability to see where the kingdom can grow and where it is currently growing. We judge and delimit according to our values, culture, and what's familiar to us where instead the kingdom should unfurl. If you hang on to the hope of being able to control where and how the kingdom grows, you will likely be discouraged by the outcomes.

In these parables, Jesus foreshadows the directive that He gives each one of us: to take a humble posture and follow Him. Following Jesus is a counterintuitive journey, and the kingdom is cultivated by willing people who give up their preconceived notions and follow Jesus into unimagined places where holy things grow in ways you least expect them to. What we see throughout Mark's Gospel is God's kingdom showing up in strange places with very little assistance from the disciples. As we walk with Jesus in this world, an awareness of God's kingdom growing in our midst should give us comfort and show us the way forward. We don't have to figure it out or control

///

As we walk with Jesus in this world, an awareness of God's kingdom growing in our midst should give us comfort and show us the way forward.

\\\

it. We need to discover it, bear witness to it, nurture it, and cultivate it, and when it reveals itself, celebrate it.

CREATING SPACE AND LETTING THE KINGDOM GROW

My friend Bobby builds incredible furniture. He takes old discarded pallets, tears them apart, and builds some of the nicest Adirondack chairs I have ever sat in. But Bobby doesn't just build furniture, he does it with friendships he has developed through his job as the director of street outreach for the local gospel mission.

For years, Bobby was the youth services director. As some of the boys he met in our neighborhood began growing into men, he saw the challenges that kept many of these young men from gainful employment: lack of formal education, fragmented families, street activity, and a tough economy have all limited their opportunity to dream about and realize something more. They have been labeled *delinquent*, *gang-involved*, and far worse. So Bobby decided to take wood pallets — labeled as good for nothing, dumped in alleys around the city — and repurpose them. And as these young men participate in this work, they are seeing their lives being repurposed as well.

Bobby knew it was not enough to give these guys job training, he knew they needed to be known and affirmed in their ability to reimagine their lives in a community. So Bobby not only builds, he listens, asks questions, and cultivates. He comes with an expectation that these men are thoughtful and creative. They just need to be given a chance, to be listened to, and have someone to walk with them.

Every time Bobby works with them, they do demolition on the pallets. In the process, they begin to deconstruct some of the fables that have shaped their lives. As they build, they see old things that were once purposeless recreated into furniture that looks nothing like the pallets once pulled from a dumpster.

Every Thursday they gather over lunch and talk through a story or Scripture, and the young men are in charge of drawing meaning from the text, thinking through the application, and giving their understanding of how it applies.

I am known by many in my community as Pops, and to Bobby, I have always been called Doc. These titles are a huge honor. They come with enormous responsibility, and I do not take them lightly. So sometimes old Doc gets to sit with the hardworking men around this lunchroom and listen to these young men's exegesis.

One Tuesday we sat around a common table and talked about Plato's Allegory (or Parable) of the Cave. In the story, Plato imagines people who live their lives chained to the wall of a cave. As others walk by the entrance of the shell that holds them, a shadow or reflection is cast on the cave wall. The chained people only know the world through the shadows on the cave wall. One prisoner escapes and sees reality is not comprised of the shadows — the escapee sees a whole new world. Upon his return, he begins to tell the story to his imprisoned friends, but the story he testifies to is so threatening that the one who has seen the exterior of the cave is killed by his captive community.

At this point I ask you, who reads Plato with young men from the south side of our city? Who believes that this soil is worthy of these deep philosophical seeds? Who believes philosophical thought can grow in the Rainier Valley?

So the men began to retell the story and argue over its meaning. At times the conversation wandered, and it began to feel like modern jazz—I was left wondering if we were going to get back to the original melody. Bobby seemed OK with the conversation running down rabbit trails.

As we sat there, I asked what this story had to do with the 98118 zip code and 118 Design (the name of Bobby's furniture company) that brings these guys together. After a long pause, one young man courageously spoke up. "When I was running those streets, I thought I was a true man, and I had plenty of women." Everyone laughed honestly but with a certain amount of discomfort. Darius went on, "My girlfriend would be in the other room, and I would bring girls home. Then we had a baby, and I began to be a real father and tried to be a good, well, husband." More awkward laughter. "What's amazing is," Darius went on to explain, "when I let go of that hard image and started to love my kids and my wife, those guys who I thought were my friends harassed me, made fun of me, told me I was soft!" Bobby encouraged the guys to think about how Darius's story connected to the cave? Aaron spoke up, "Oh, can't you see?" Aaron explains matter-of-factly, "When you start living honest like real men, people that believe the lie don't want you to make it, 'cause then they gotta live in the light, too!"

I have never heard Plato broken down so well. What I see happening at 118 Design is more than reclaiming scrap wood. I see a group of men discovering the seeds of the kingdom growing in and revealed in their desires, and those seeds are cultivated by the guy who thought old pallets shouldn't be tossed away. That what looks like scrap wood can be reconstructed into some of the most beautiful lawn furniture I have ever sat on. Do we have eyes to see where this kingdom grows? We can't own it. We can't figure it out. It grows in crazy places and is completely beyond our control. But when we see it growing we can cultivate it. It grows in crazy places and with those we might not expect.

CHAPTER 5

REALLY GOOD REASONS NOT TO GIVE

It's one of most familiar Bible stories in our culture. The phrase "Good Samaritan" is woven into the moral fabric of our society. It has come to define someone who performs a spontaneous act of incredible kindness. But as we look more closely at the story Jesus tells in Luke, we find far more than a nice guy caring for someone who's a little down on his luck. It's a radical story that gives us a starting place to examine more deeply how it is we are meant to care for the world. It challenges us to consider who is deserving of our help, and what "good" helping looks like. And it asks us to pay attention to the behavior of people who aren't much different, in many ways, than you and me.

The story begins with a lawyer. He comes to Jesus and asks, "What must I do to inherit eternal life?" (Luke 10:25). It's a fair question, one that is asked more than once throughout the biblical text: What does it mean to be righteous before God, to do the right thing? The answer Jesus gives draws on two sections of Scripture, Deuteronomy 6:5 and the holiness codes found in Leviticus

(19:17–18, 33–34). Jesus invites the lawyer to give the first answer by asking, "What is written in the law?" The lawyer responds correctly stating, "Love the LORD your God with all your heart and with all your soul and with all strength" (Deuteronomy 6:5). And then he adds, "Love your neighbor as yourself" (Leviticus 19:18). The lawyer follows up with a clarifying question, "And who is my neighbor?" (Luke 10:29). He appears to be pondering the practical implications of this idea of loving the people around him. Maybe he senses that this "loving other people" stuff might get messy real quick, and, like all of us, he wants to know where he can place parameters on this love.

Then Jesus tells a simple but groundbreaking story in Luke 10:30–37:

> In reply Jesus said: "A man was going down from Jerusalem to Jericho, when he was attacked by robbers. They stripped him of his clothes, beat him and went away, leaving him half dead. A priest happened to be going down the same road, and when he saw the man, he passed by on the other side. So too, a Levite, when he came to the place and saw him, passed by on the other side. But a Samaritan, as he traveled, came where the man was; and when he saw him, he took pity on him. He went to him and bandaged his wounds, pouring on oil and wine. Then he put the man on his own donkey, brought him to an inn and took care of him. The next day he took out two denarii and gave them to the innkeeper. 'Look after him,' he said, 'and when I return, I will reimburse you for any extra expense you may have.' Which of these three do you think was a neighbor to the man who fell into the hands

of robbers?" The expert in the law replied, "The one who had
mercy on him." Jesus told him, "Go and do likewise."

Let's start with a few details about the story's characters and context. First of all, the priest and Levite aren't bad people. They, like the Pharisees, are legitimate keepers of the law: religious leaders in good standing in their community. They are advocates for a standard of righteousness that is clear and definitive. They represent the people and occupy a sacred space between a holy God and His flock. Many of us are familiar with the Gospel writers' depictions of the religious leaders' opposition to Jesus. They've been penned the "bad" guys. It's difficult to listen to the story without some element of contempt for these characters — but they would have been well-respected by Jesus' listeners.

Second, at the time that Jesus told this story, the law upheld by the priest and the Levite had been completely violated by the Samaritans. These Samaritans had a conflicted relationship with their Jewish relatives since the time of the Babylonian exile. They consisted of the two tribes left when most of Judah was taken into captivity. Without leadership they had taken liberty with much of what we now call the Pentateuch (the first five books of our Bible), and this created an intense tribal conflict. They were the scourge of the Jewish people. Already we see the story becoming more complicated than it first appears. The lawyer asks Jesus about the legal requirements outlining who he's responsible to help, and Jesus doesn't hesitate to pick the most unusual suspects and put them in the "wrong" place in the story. The righteous become violators of God's law, and vice versa.

The setting of the story is another important component. The road Jesus chose was a dangerous, 17-mile stretch of desolate highway

*/// Serving others is not as simple . . . First, we have to wade through our knee-jerk reactions. *

from Jerusalem to Jericho. It was infamous for thieves and marauders. Jesus' listeners would have been well aware of this, and of the potential risks of the situation were they to come across a wounded man on this road. I'm struck by the many good reasons someone might have had to refuse to help a man in distress in such a dangerous place. Jesus paints an extreme picture. A simple question about a neighbor quickly becomes a high-stakes scenario of great moral complexity.

The text states that the man on the side of the road is naked. The story doesn't mention who he is or where he comes from. He could be a Jewish community member in good standing, or, just as easily, a sinner, maybe a tax collector who has manipulated and stolen from his neighbors. He could be a law-breaking Samaritan, for that matter. Whatever the case, there is nothing about him — certainly nothing he is wearing — to clarify his status or position. I'm sure that as the lawyer listened to the story, he wondered to himself, maybe before he could help it: "Is this guy worth saving?"

Or perhaps the man lying there naked is a decoy. Like so many roads I've traveled around the world, it wasn't safe to stop on the road to Jericho, especially when you were alone. Someone could be setting a trap. The priest and the Levite have no way of knowing if others are watching them, waiting for them to stop. Should they choose to help, become vulnerable themselves, and risk robbery — or worse?

The story also says the wounded man is near death. From a distance, perhaps he appears dead. Nobody wants to touch a dead body, particularly not a priest or a Levite. They might be on their way to Jerusalem to make sacrifices for the people. If they were to touch the man and find him dead, they would have to undergo an extensive cleansing process. Or, if they know that the man is "near dead," perhaps they are asking themselves whether the man can be saved. What if he dies on the way to seeking help? Is he worth taking the risk? Again, there would be complex purifying rituals that the priest and Levite would be obligated to perform. In their role serving the community, dead bodies were something to be avoided.

Finally, and very importantly, everyone knew the road to Jericho was dangerous. Common sense meant taking the necessary precautions for the journey. The priest and Levite, and those listening to Jesus' story, might have questioned why the naked man was traveling alone in the first place. Had he been carrying something that was valuable? Perhaps his predicament was his fault. Do you stop and help someone who is culpable for the mess they're in? Do you put your own life in jeopardy for the foolish choices of another?

The dynamics of this story highlight the often-complicated implications of helping another person — especially a stranger. Serving others is not as simple as throwing someone who has obviously been victimized on the back of your donkey. First, we have to wade through our knee-jerk reactions: Who are we helping? Do we owe these people anything? What is the likelihood that we can make a lasting impact in their lives? Are we helping innocent victims, or have they brought their present situation upon themselves?

I'm just speculating about what the priest and Levite are thinking, of course. But they probably do have some really good reasons not to help the man. Jesus, the master storyteller, allows them to behave like any of us might. For myriad reasons, they choose to walk on the other side of the road.

But if the priest and the Levite have good reasons not to help out a naked, half-dead man lying in the road, then the Samaritan has even

///
The farther away you stand, the easier it is to dismiss his humanity.
**

better ones. If the victim is Jewish, the Samaritan owes him nothing. No law calls him to responsibility, and he has no cause to behave toward the Jewish people as neighbors. They certainly haven't acted as neighbors to his people.

But this is exactly what he does. Though the broken, vulnerable man could be a decoy in an elaborate trap, the Samaritan makes himself vulnerable, too. No one — and I would bet my house on this — no one would stop and help the Samaritan if he were the one found robbed and beaten. Yet he puts the man on his own donkey, slowing his progress. He opens himself up to being victimized himself.

Jesus uses the character of a "lawbreaker" to guide the lawyer through a case study that forces him to judge the action of an unrighteous Samaritan. And that action is to move close. The Samaritan, we learn in Luke 10:34, "went to him."

Let's consider this phrase. Unlike the priest and the Levite, the Samaritan moves toward the man. This is the beginning point of any loving act. On a literal level, the farther away from the victim of a robbery or an assault one moves, the easier it becomes to assume that person is already dead, past help. The easier it becomes to conclude he looks nothing like you and has no connection to the predicaments you might find yourself in. The farther away you stand, the easier it is to dismiss his humanity and assume that because he's naked, he's just a body — no longer a person, but a corpse. Beyond saving.

But the Samaritan moves toward the man. He gets close enough to see and hear the victim's impossible situation. He gets close enough to look straight at him and absorb something of his pain and disgrace, the violation of one who has been robbed of his humanity, stripped of his value, beaten down physically, emotionally, and spiritually, and left for dead.

As we talk about doing justice and loving the world, this is a distinction worth paying attention to — coming near versus keeping oneself apart. The farther away we stand from those in need, the easier it is to blame, accuse, or dismiss them, or simply say they're not anything like me and have little to do with my problems. It's easier to decide that those in need are not salvageable or the cost is too great.

As I mentioned earlier, one of the unforeseen challenges I found in serving marginalized young people in Seattle was constantly negotiating the "good reasons not to give" mentality of supporters who were concerned, often legitimately, that the people they were helping might never reach their standard of success. It was difficult to persuade them that success might look very different from the dominant culture's definition, and that was OK. At times, the resistance came in the form of accusations and laying blame, faulting people for their pre-dicament and for choosing

///

Success might look very different from the dominant culture's definition, and that was OK.

\\\

the lifestyles that they had. But mostly, it sounded like good reasons not to give, reasons I am sometimes tempted to rely on myself.

If we offer help to these people, what guarantee do we have that they will become success stories? Don't you know how many times a kid addicted to drugs or alcohol gets treatment and then relapses? The last thing we want to do is put a homeless kid on our own donkey, only to get halfway to success and have that young person return to the street because that's where his real friends are.

In our culture, we hate sending alcoholics to treatment again and again. And we don't want to rescue a young girl from prostitution only to see her run back into the arms of an abusive relationship.

My point is this: the kinds of questions we ask ourselves about whether our help is warranted or not are the same ones that seem to be running through the minds of the characters in the story of the Good Samaritan. The complications that Jesus intentionally placed in the narrative hit close to home: Is it worth my time to stop and help? Do the people I'm helping deserve my kindness? Will they be able to meet my standard of success, or will I carry them halfway to help only to have them die on the way?

I'm not saying these aren't understandable, even useful concerns. Carefully thinking through ways to help that will increase a person's likelihood of moving forward into hope and healing is vitally important. Evaluating the effectiveness of those strategies is also critical. Helping people become personally responsible and empowering them to make good choices is crucial for lasting transformation. I spent my previous book attempting to describe how best to serve young people who are in a tough spot. But what I *am* saying is that the farther away we stand from the problem, the more we lack the ability to see the problem's complexity. Helping is complicated, and if we keep our distance, the easier it will be to turn to simple answers or throw our hands up in frustration, believing we've done all we can do. So my encouragement to all of us is this: If we are going to love the world, really love it, we have to get close enough to see how messy and complicated loving people really is. It might cost us something. We might have to change how we define success. We might find that the choices we see people making that seem foolish at a distance make more sense as we draw near and hear more of their story. Getting closer might also reveal something in ourselves that isn't that great to look at. It might expose the truth that the victim is more like us than we were ever willing to admit.

HE WENT TO HIM

The words "He went to him" (Luke 10:34) move the Samaritan beyond caution and concern. They also beautifully echo the journey of Jesus toward a hurting humanity, invoked in the first chapter of the Gospel of John.

> *The Word became flesh and made his dwelling among us.*
> *We have seen his glory, the glory of the one and only Son,*
> *who came from the Father, full of grace and truth.*
>
> —JOHN 1:14

Every Tuesday night, for two and a half years, a group of incredible young leaders gathered at mine and Linda's home. We talked about our lives, and what it means to serve youth and families in hard places. We talked about community, beauty, and justice. We would share a meal together, have a conversation, and experience the Eucharist. It began as an informal gathering where, regardless of your faith perspective, you were invited as a full participant. No one had to be an expert. Anyone could lead the dialogue. You didn't have to have a brilliant answer. You just needed to come up with a good question, a "beauti-ful question," as many of my friends in the Street Psalms community would say — an open-ended question that starts with something particular and moves to a bigger idea. A good question that you don't have the answer to makes room for many really good answers.

///

Grace and mercy say, "Relax, it's OK; you can't fix a stinking thing!"

**

During one Tuesday night conversation, my son Ben and his buddy Ellrol wanted to discuss grace, mercy, and karma. Ben and Ellrol invited all of us to respond to the questions: "Have you ever felt grace, and, if so, when did you feel it?" and "Did you ever feel like giving it away?" As we engaged with these questions, we tried very hard to get to the root of how we can live into the revolutionary reality illuminated in the story of the Good Samaritan — a story about a radical act of unconditional love and mercy.

During the discussion, someone brought up John 1:14—"The Word became flesh and made his dwelling among us"—which stirred up more questions: "What do we experience when Jesus, full of grace, comes toward us?" "What does it feel like?" "What does it look like in our neighborhood?" "If karma means getting what you deserve, how are grace and mercy different from that?" As I sat and listened to the responses, I felt the soil of the conversation being gently sifted, revealing precious stones. Everyone had something brilliant to add. It was through this discussion, this remarkable moment, and others like it that we began to realize that we were much better off trying to answer these questions together rather than on our own.

Grace and mercy in the story of God are incredible ideas, but, at times, a little confusing — perhaps disorienting. Grace and mercy, to be what they are, meet us at our worst. They interact with the lowest part of our soul and our humanness. My sin and shame tell me to run toward perfection, plant my flag there, and persuade myself that I'm OK. Perfection declares that everything is going to get better. Grace tells us that it might not get better in the way we want it to, but that is also OK.

In U2's song, "Grace," Bono sings, "Grace makes beauty out of ugly things" and "Grace finds beauty in everything." Grace and mercy wade into the middle of our garbage. They pool up in the lowest places. They wait patiently for us to admit we can't fix anything. We can't make it right. Grace tells us we don't get what we deserve, and mercy comes along and gives us everything we don't deserve. But be careful — as recipients of grace and mercy, we also don't get what we've earned. So say good-bye to all those heavenly crowns. In our human reality, we feel we need to strive, to succeed, to separate ourselves from just *being* and work with everything we've got to *be better*. Grace and mercy say, "Relax, it's OK; you can't fix a stinking thing!" They whisper, "It's over. Everything has been taken care of."

This is a big concept to sit with. What if it *is* over, really over? And how would we behave if we truly believed that? Someone in the group the night of our discussion about grace and mercy asked, "What if grace really has come, and we're all OK?" Together, we tried to imagine this new paradigm. We asked more questions: What if Jesus' incarnation has ushered in the reality that *all* things really are becoming new? What if, in God coming to us like the Samaritan going to the broken and beaten man, He is declaring that He has no beef with us? What if this is how grace and mercy behave? What if Jesus came to reveal that *we* are the ones who have a problem with God, but that God is not mad at us — that He truly came not to condemn the world, but to save it? What if the real problem is that even though *we* can't make ourselves better, we use up our energy trying to do just that, and end up spending our lives in blame and accusation? Grace says no one needs to be blamed or accused anymore. What if it's over — *really over* — because of grace?

Here's where some would say: Ron and his friends are Universalists!

I have to defer to Jürgen Moltmann here, who claims that Jesus was crucified outside the gate — the implication is all those outside have access. The crucified God outside the gate decides who is in and who is out. I don't think it's my job to make that call, one way or the other.

///

He said that a bowl of rice, a glass of water, and a place to use the restroom is a basic human right, and who is he to refuse a human being this right?

**

But I do think we are to live as if grace is real and available to everyone. As followers of Christ, we believe that when Jesus entered our world, grace opened up a new space for us to dwell in — one without rancor or condemnation. What if we who believe in this grace simply extend it to the world? You are forgiven! I no longer have to blame anyone, even myself! What if the mission of the church is simply to bear witness to how Jesus has shown us grace, and act out this grace in the world?

That could be really good news.

WHO IS MY NEIGHBOR?

At the end of the Good Samaritan story, Jesus asks a straightforward question: "Which of these . . . was a neighbor?" (Luke 10:36). The lawyer now has a choice to make. Does he align himself with his law-abiding community, with the priest and Levite who have status and spiritual authority? Or does he align himself with the epitome of lawbreakers who goes to the man and cares for him at great expense to himself?

The lawyer answers correctly. He simply states, "The one who showed him mercy" (NLT). Hosea 6:6 echoes in my mind every time I read the lawyer's answer: "For I desire mercy, not sacrifice."

But the simplicity of Jesus' question and the lawyer's answer disguises a sophisticated rhetorical reframing of the question "Who is my neighbor?" In verse 29, the lawyer asks the question as a point of clarification. In this instance, *neighbor* is a noun. Basically, he wants to know which people in his life he is being commanded to call his neighbor. What's the definition? Is it about relationship, values, or geographic proximity?

But in verse 36, Jesus inverts the question. No longer is it about neighbor in proximity, *Who is my neighbor?* It is a question of action, *Who acts like a neighbor?*

The call of justice is the call to *be* a neighbor — to *act* like a neighbor, to love as if *everyone* is my neighbor. The question becomes, "What roads are we willing to cross for the sake of grace, mercy, and justice? How far are we willing to go?"

Recently I ate at a Muslim-owned restaurant in my neighborhood with Bobby, my friend who turns old pallets into beautiful furniture. We eat there a lot. As we sat there, a filthy young man came in and used the bathroom, then left. Bobby thought he recognized the young man and asked our friends who owned the café if they knew the guy. The owner said no, but quickly told us that didn't matter. He has instructed his employees that no one who is thirsty is to be refused a drink of water, and anyone who is hungry can have a bowl of rice. Anyone who needs to use the restroom is welcome to do so. He went on to clarify that even if the "customer" smells bad, they can use the restroom. He acknowledged that sometimes a smelly man can make for a smelly bathroom, but that cleaning up the lavatory is really no problem at all. Then he said that a bowl of rice, a glass of water, and a place to use the restroom is a basic human right, and who is he to refuse a human being this right?

Never in my life had I heard of a business owner doing such a thing. I had seen signs that read, "We reserve the right to refuse business to anyone" and "Bathrooms are for customers only" — both within a proprietor's rights. But I'd never seen one that said, "Humans deserve these basic rights." Unheard of. As we sat there, we were overwhelmed by the owner's sense of mercy — overwhelming, unbridled mercy.

"The one who showed him mercy" (NLT) is the lawyer's final answer. It's really quite simple. It's also the most difficult thing I can imagine. We are asked to extend mercy and grace to the world. We are asked to let go of our good reasons not to give. If we really believe that the story of the Christian faith is about God's grace coming near us in the life of Jesus, maybe all we are being asked to do is extend to the world the measure of mercy and grace that we have been given.

CHAPTER 6

LOVING MERCY, DOING JUSTICE

A few years ago I sat in a graduate school classroom in Boston, having recently been accepted into the doctor of ministry program at Gordon-Conwell Theological Seminary. But I should be totally honest — I spent no time on the Gordon-Conwell campus, and on that particular day I wasn't sitting in a formal classroom. I was in the Jamaica Plain neighborhood of Boston, in an old funeral parlor that had been converted into the classrooms and offices for Gordon-Conwell's Center for Urban Ministerial Education program. For those of you who think there's not much of a difference between seminary and a cemetery, I'm sure you're already laughing. But this was a lively group!

I was in my first residency working toward a doctor of ministry in complex urban settings. We were studying the city and how faith works itself out in heterogeneous urban settings. I had purposely chosen this seminary not only for the degree and the curriculum but also for the students. Baptist, Pentecostal, Methodist, and Orthodox Christians were crammed into the little classroom, folding themselves into desks two sizes too small. My colleagues were

African American, Dominican, and Anglo, folks from Ecuador, Nicaragua, Texas, Boston, and Miami. They were social workers, probation officers, pastors, and drug counselors. It was as diverse a classroom as any I had been in before.

///

You think you can have one without the other? . . .

You can't.

**

We laughed a lot. Many of my classmates were born preachers, so we all talked a lot. We had to learn to listen. We argued sometimes, usually while laughing at each other. The Baptist guy wondered if the Orthodox brothers were saved. The Pentecostals told the Methodists they needed to work on their holiness. One day we had a typical theological scuffle over this question: "Which is more important — righteousness or justice?" Some people argued that you can't do good in the world until you get the God thing right: righteousness. Others contended that you have to start by diving right in and living out the practical expression of God's love: justice. It was a heated and lively debate.

One of my new friends, a Latino guy who isn't a native English speaker, was a little confused by the conversation. He leaned over and asked, "What are we fighting about?" I told him I would explain when we took a break. A few minutes later, Miguel and I were talking over a cup of coffee. I wondered how to explain this deep-rooted conflict in the church (at least the church in North America). I started at what I thought was the beginning.

"Miguel, from what I vaguely remember from a graduate class at Pepperdine, this kind of thing got started before the Civil War in the United States," I began. "We had a lot of stuff going on. There was a desire to end slavery, and a substantial part of the church was also driven by a very scientific apologetic. So on one side of the aisle, we were concerned with social issues, and on the other side, we wanted to be able to prove what was fundamental to our faith. We fell into an Enlightenment trap of trying to 'out science' science for the sake of faith. We tried to prove the Bible was perfect, correct, and credible by scientific standards. A lot of people felt that it was important not to become distracted by issues that weren't central to that cause — things that weren't 'fundamental' to faith. Other people challenged that and asked how the church could ignore such a horrible and pervasive social issue like slavery. So the labels 'social gospel' and 'fundamentalist' began to be used. The social gospel side focused on creating justice, and the fundamentalist group focused on pursuing righteousness."

"Oh!" Miguel interrupted. "I see what your problem is."

"My problem?" Wasn't I the one doing the explaining?

Miguel went on: "You North Americans have a language problem. You have separated the words *justice* and *righteousness*. In Spanish there's only one word for justice and righteousness: *justicia*," Miguel laughed. "You think you can have one without the other? Those of us who speak and understand Spanish know you can't. That's your problem!"

I've thought about that conversation a lot since then. Is it really that simple? Have we created a division that doesn't need to exist? The act of doing justice in the world can't be as simple as changing our vocabulary. Or can it? What would it mean if we were able to reframe justice and righteousness as being far more connected than we are used to treating them?

A few years later, I read David J. Bosch's incredible book *Transforming Mission*, and discovered that a Greek word used throughout the New Testament to describe God's justice — *dikaiosyne* — means, in fact, both "justice" and "righteousness." Bosch claims that *dikaiosyne* poses the same language problem for English that my friend Miguel had pointed out to me. It can mean God's justice toward us (mercy). But it can also mean righteousness (a spiritual attribute of God's, and a quality we can share). It can define a person's "right" relationship with God *as well as* our right relationships with each other.

Looking back, it seems like much of our fight in the seminary class stemmed from the limitations of our language, and the fact that we hadn't fully understood the connections between justice and righteousness, especially as they are manifested in the word *dikaiosyne*.

Historical and theological debate is packed with controversy over these sorts of "hot button" words. Maybe our oversight that day in seminary was the result of our upbringing in a hyper-individualized North American culture. We understood righteousness primarily as a quality that God bestows on each of us, in a personal, one-on-one relationship. Justice was about doing good in the community. What if our problem comprehending the full meaning of justice and righteousness was truly that: *our* problem? If my friend Miguel and David Bosch are right, how might a new understanding of these concepts change how we respond to our world?

BLESSED ARE THOSE WHO HUNGER AND THIRST FOR RIGHTEOUSNESS/JUSTICE

I was talking through this idea a while back with my colleague Kris Rocke, one of my ordained clergy friends in the Street Psalms community. He pointed out to me that the King James Bible uses the term *righteousness* over the word *justice* in the Sermon on the Mount. Think about the significance of this deliberate choice. If I'm a king and I want loyal subjects, I want them to be concerned with righteousness. I want them to want to be good and to obey my decrees. It can feel good, after all, to be in right standing with authority. But if you call your citizens to pursue justice, to consider how their relationships affect their fellow citizens, they might begin questioning the laws of the monarchy. Could it be that the word *justice* was avoided here because it might have threatened the king's system and potentially put the king's power in jeopardy?

Some translations of this passage have started to replace the word *righteousness* with *justice*. The New Living Translation, for instance, reads: "God blesses those who hunger and thirst for *justice*, for they will be satisfied" (Matthew 5:6, author's emphasis).

How does it change our reading of Matthew 5:6 when we replace the word *righteousness* with the word *justice*? What are the implications for our relationships with others? What happens when prioritizing relationships comes at the expense of obeying authority and institutions?

WHAT DOES THE BIBLE MEAN BY JUSTICE?

All of this begs the question — what does justice actually mean in the social and theological context of Scripture? In his book *Biblical Ethics and Social Change*, Stephen Charles Mott walks his reader through the rich complexities of Christian responsibility in the world. One of the pillars of his argument involves the distinction between *distributive justice* and *retributive justice*. Mott claims, "In atonement God's righteousness (distributive justice) overcomes God's wrath (retributive justice)." The creative justice of God does not preserve the status quo but rather distributes opportunity for those who are oppressed. Biblical justice, according to Mott, attacks the causes of suffering. He then concludes that biblical justice — *distributive justice* — addresses the causes of suffering in our world at their very root by leveling the playing field for all those who have not benefited from the status quo, who have, in fact, been oppressed by it. What Mott seems to be saying is that the theme of *retributive justice* — you reap what you sow, you get what you deserve — is overshadowed in the biblical text by a righteous God who acts justly toward the creation He loves by working to restore relationship and bring about full flourishing for all human beings. Mott attacks the presuppositions of the "what would Jesus do" movement. The more theologically accurate question regarding ethics then becomes, "What has the grace of God, revealed in Jesus, empowered *me* to do?"

Mott goes on to explain how this grace experienced is then walked out in love, justice, and the kingdom of God. Mott says justice brings the future reign of God into the present. If it is true that righteousness and justice are intimately connected, and justice in Scripture has a whole lot to do with giving people equal opportunity and agency, then what does righteousness truly look like for us?

It could be argued that the Bible is saying the way we treat the person we love the least — *justice* — is the way we love God the most — *righteousness*. By living with a language that uses separate words for *justice* and *righteousness*, perhaps we have failed to see that how we care for others, especially those whom society deems "unclean" or unworthy, is vital to what it means to be Christian. What if justice is an act of grace-filled restoration that welcomes the reign of God on earth as it is in heaven — a reign that sets a table for every person and moves out into the world seeking out those who have been abandoned?

THE KINGDOM OF GOD AND THE AMERICAN DREAM

In the world we live in, institutions of power define the vision of reality that most people accept as the norm — the status quo — and determine who will receive access to resources and who will at some level be denied access. This is contrary to God's vision of justice. Justice is the kingdom of God active among us. It challenges the way things are and reveals how things should be. It lays bare the question, "What version of reality have we unthinkingly accepted and are being asked to let go of?"

Certain values imbedded in our cultural narrative lull us into believing that our current reality is just the way things are and limit this new vision of the way things could be. We even endorse and dress up that reality with sayings about God that, quite frankly, God never said. Here are a few examples:

- *God helps those who help themselves. (Yet, "In God we trust.")*

- *Cleanliness is next to godliness, because you've got to look like money to make money.*

- *And, of course, since God helps those who help themselves, anyone can achieve anything because where there's a will there's a way. Everyone can be a*

self-made man or woman, independent heroes who
pull themselves up by their own bootstraps.

These and other truisms shape not only us but also our relationships and our view of God. They serve as a framework for the way we think life should be lived.

///
As you read the biblical narrative you'll see very little of the bootstrap mentality.
\\\

With these ideas imbedded so deeply in our collective consciousness, it's easy to see why social problems like poverty are treated as individual rather than systemic issues. If poverty is the problem of individuals, then it is the responsibility of the poor to regroup and change their circumstances through their individual choices. The saying "God helps those who help themselves" stems from the influence of the Protestant work ethic. This idea seems to be the foundation of much of our dominant culture's psyche, even among Christ-followers. By default, we tend to believe that God supplies the extra effort to *our* effort. There is nothing wrong with hard work. But in this text we are reminded it is God who initiates the activity, not us.

And there is nothing wrong with self-initiative; in fact, it's a very good thing. Self-empowerment enables us to take ownership of our past and allows us to move toward the future God has for us. But as you read the biblical narrative you'll see very little of the bootstrap mentality or stories about people who somehow deserve God's intervention according to their cleanliness or effort. Rather, what we read over and over is the story of people who desperately need God's intervention and, most often, instead take matters into their own hands, their fear and lack of faith getting the best of them, sabotaging the plans of the Almighty — all the Abrahams, Jacobs, and Davids who move forward on their own and end up wondering what went wrong.

But what if the church were able to imagine something beyond the idea that we get what we deserve and have worked for?

Walter Brueggemann, in *A Social Reading of the Old Testament*, claims that one of the primary tasks of the prophetic voice is to speak to institutions of social power. The prophet urges us to envision another system, an alternative to the way things have always been, a way of relating to the world that is based on a different power structure — that of the kingdom.

It's the work of the prophet to initiate a rereading of reality and to propose an alternative to the norms of the dominant cultural perspective. It's the prophet's call to reveal the way in which the powers of this world conflict with the way power works in God's kingdom. The prophet bears witness to where the kingdom grows and what it produces. The prophet gives hope to a world that believes life cannot be different than it is.

///

Mercy . . . stands in utter opposition to the idea that we should be able to make it on our own. . . .

Mercy is ministry to the most broken parts of our community and the most broken parts of ourselves. . . .

Mercy is love extended to the world, even if those we love never meet our standard of success.

**

One of my favorite passages that exemplifies this is Micah 6:1–8. The story goes something like this: God, through the prophet Micah, has brought an accusation against ancient Israel. Just so they know that it's serious, Micah explains the charge using a legal metaphor. In verses 1–2, the Lord brings a case against Israel — essentially, God takes the ancient Hebrews to court. The mountains that have over-shadowed the people for generations are God's witnesses. What are the charges revealed earlier in the book? The poor have been treated like slaughtered animals (Micah 3:2). The rich have stolen land and coveted fields; they have oppressed a man and taken his house (2:2).

What would it be like to hear God tell you that you are oppressing the poor and slaughtering them like animals? The Hebrew people have seen what God does with oppressors. He took their oppressors and their horses and washed them away with the sea.

In Micah 6:3–4, God asks the people why they would behave like this and reminds them that, contrary to popular belief, they are not a people who have pulled themselves up by their own bootstraps. The mountains have seen it all. They know the history God lays out. The Hebrews are a people rescued and preserved by the hand of God. The ancients can't take credit for what they've done. In the context of the rest of Micah, the Lord seems to be asking this pointed question: why wouldn't you extend the same grace to those around you?

It is here in the story that we move back to the dilemma of choosing between *righteousness* and *justice*. Micah 6:6–7 gives us the voices of people defending themselves. "What do you want from us? Our worship is right! We have the right form, we have this part correct, don't we?" Then the defense becomes extreme: "What do you want, God?" the Hebrews ask. "Do you want our firstborn?" I've always wondered if this is a reference to Abraham and Isaac. Here is the question at the heart of their questions: "Is this what it will take for us to be right with God?" They've climbed the spiritual ladder of success, relying on form and ritual, only to find out they've been climbing the wrong ladder.

Now we come to Micah 6:8. It's here that right worship of the Almighty — righteousness — and right relationship with those around us — justice — are brought together in the most beautiful way. Micah ties together Deuteronomy 6:5 ("Love the Lord your God with all your heart") and Leviticus 19:18 ("Love your neighbor as yourself"), and introduces the command in a very specific way: "He has shown you, O mortal, what is good. And what does the Lord require of you?" This portion of the verse serves not only as a call to behave differently, but also as a model for *how* to set about behaving differently — we are to imitate God's example of justice and mercy, and to do so in humble relationship with Him. This, according to the prophet Micah, is true worship.

DEFINING THE TERMS

Mercy

Mercy is best defined as faithfulness to others. Mercy is love without condition. Mercy is not getting what one deserves. It stands in utter opposition to the idea that we should be able to make it on our own. Mercy says that what we make on our own is often a mess. Mercy is ministry to the most broken parts of our community and the most broken parts of ourselves. Mercy is love extended to the world, even if those we love never meet our standard of success.

Mercy reflects a God who is willing to abide in the most broken parts of the world. Being flesh and blood with people. *For* people. Following the example of Jesus who became flesh and dwelt among us (John 1:14), we as Christians have been called by God to build relationships. We must be with those who feel they have no place, build trusting relationships, and care for people through acts of

///
Justice doesn't give voice to the voiceless. It cries out for ears for the earless.
\\\

authentic love and grace that nurture community and connection.

Extending mercy means that we awaken to the fact that the church has been called by God to feed the hungry and clothe the naked. Feeding and clothing the orphan (Deuteronomy 10:18) means meeting primary needs, which opens up space for introspection — essential to the stirring of the soul toward deeper relationship with God and others. Mercy simply gives without condition. No requirements, no expectations. It doesn't give us what we deserve; it offers what we need in spite of what we deserve. Mercy exemplifies the love of God. And I think God is asking us to extend the same mercy that God has extended to us.

Justice

If mercy can be described as ministering to people, then justice is ministering with people. If mercy stands up for people, then justice stands with them. Justice is an empowering force that gives people a platform to speak truth to powerful entities who have lost sight of it. I've always hated the phrase "a voice for the voiceless." The marginalized don't need a voice. They have a voice. What they don't have are ears willing to listen to their voice. Justice doesn't give voice to the voiceless. It cries out for ears for the earless.

Justice protects the identity and humanity of each person created by God. It builds confidence and self-esteem. Jeremiah 1 describes how God knew Jeremiah when he was in his mother's womb and had plans for his future. Justice stands with people as they find out who they were created to be. It helps people discover personal agency and community power. And it is exemplified through community connection, solidarity, and friendship. The work of justice is rooted, first and foremost, in believing that our friendship with God empowers all of our work and life. And this nearness to God calls us into the space of friendship and solidarity with those we serve with, knowing that while we all come from different places, we stand in the same place with God, and deserve the same opportunities to help us become more fully who we are.

Justice treats humankind as we were created to be treated. Justice lays bare the disparities in this world and labors and aches for the kingdom of God to come. It acts out a vision of how the world ought to be for everyone to see. No wonder Dr. Martin Luther King Jr. called justice "love in public."

///

Humility recognizes you can't do justice right until you listen to those who have been treated unjustly.

**

Humility

As I researched this passage in Micah in preparation for a sermon, I came across a couple of interesting points concerning the phrase "walk humbly." First, there is no English word that can encompass it. It's too comprehensive. Second, the sweeping quality of humility suggested in the passage is not a third category alongside mercy and justice. Humility hovers over mercy and justice — an overarching way of being in the world. It allows us to experience ourselves in proper relationship to each other.

I can relate to this idea. It's one that began to sink in as I wrote my first book. I went into that project wanting to write a book about my work with kids on the street. What I quickly discovered was how much they had shaped and taught *me*. They were the face of God in my life. Humility allows us to admit that we have been shaped by our experiences — that we are who we are because of others. Humility is the willingness to admit what we don't know, even when it involves the mystery of our faith. But we follow, we believe, and we rest in the assurance that we belong — to God, and to each other.

I believe that humility is exemplified in learning to enter into diverse community. It means admitting that each one of us — coming out of our own faith tradition and social location — has blind spots. Humility recognizes you can't do justice right until you listen to those who have been treated unjustly. Humility invites other voices to the table. It embraces the vision of the culturally and economically diverse church described in Revelation 7:9. This is the church that is called to be an ambassador of reconciliation in 2 Corinthians 5. Justice is the prophet Micah declaring a kingdom where the lame are God's beloved, and the castoffs are a strong nation (Micah 4:6–7). Humility is dangerously inclusive in the name of reconciliation. It invites other opinions and makes room for the outcast and alien. It is a listening posture. Humility admits what it doesn't have and asks what it needs from God and neighbor.

Justice, Righteousness, and Relationship with God

This intimate connection between justice and righteousness appears all through our sacred text. The prophet Isaiah, fed up with so-called "righteousness" and pious acts of fasting, declares that true, authentic worship is rooted in workers' rights and food redistribution — in a word: *justice*. Isaiah 58:3–7:

Yet on the day of your fasting, you do as you please and exploit all your workers. Your fasting ends in quarreling and strife, and in striking each other with wicked fists. You cannot fast as you do today and expect your voice to be heard on high. Is this the kind of fast I have chosen, only a day for people to humble themselves? Is it only for bowing one's head like a reed and for lying in sackcloth and ashes? Is that what you call a fast, a day acceptable to the LORD? Is not this the kind of fasting I have chosen: to loose the chains of injustice and untie the cords of the yoke, to set the oppressed free and break every yoke? Is it not to share your food with the hungry and to provide the poor wanderer with shelter — when you see the naked, to clothe them?

How are all of these concepts — worship, fasting, and righteousness — connected to justice? In this way: Extending mercy acts out the story that God has come close to us. Mercy gives without condition, bearing witness to the fact that we have received without condition. Justice displays the dramatic difference between the kingdom of this world and the kingdom of our God. It gives life to a community of faith that doesn't live by the same categories adopted by this world. Lowering ourselves in humility shows us and those around us that we realize there is a God bigger than our ideas of God. This God is honored through our prayerful dependence, through our willingness to relax into the mystery of faith — a mystery that is expressed in the mutual giving of self that happens in inclusive communities.

How do we have right worship? We start by declaring that mercy *gives*, justice *stands with,* and humility *bows.*

The ancients thought, like many of us do today, that

righteousness can be grasped by getting the "right" recipe for worship or sacrifice. But what the prophet Micah declares is that there is a direct correlation between our connection to God and our connection to others.

The true evidence of God dwelling in a people is in how they relate to each other. Paul calls this the fruit of the spirit — "fruit" meaning what the tree or plant produces. The world will know the true followers of Jesus by their fruit, the evidence of the indwelling of God's spirit. Here's a picture of what that looks like:

> *But the fruit of the Spirit is love, joy, peace, forbearance, kindness, goodness, faithfulness, gentleness and self-control. Against such things there is no law.*
>
> —GALATIANS 5:22–23

I got to hear an amazing spoken word artist named Micah Bournes perform a few years back. He is a gifted young man who shared some profound things about Africa and the call of the church, but one idea in particular stuck with me. I couldn't get it out of my head and heart, and it led me to think considerably about the relationship between holiness — or righteousness — and justice. He made the statement that holiness can only really be worked out in our relationship with the other. He put this question to us: "How can you exhibit the fruit of the spirit by yourself?" Think about it. Love, peace, and kindness can only be worked out in relationship. The fruit of the spirit — the evidence of God dwelling in the human soul — is directly related to how we treat each other. We can't have righteousness without justice. *The way we treat the person we love the least is the way we love God the most.*

CHAPTER 7

FOLLOWING JESUS IN THE WAY OF THE CROSS

It was Lenten season, the 40 days the church takes before Easter to walk with Jesus toward His Passion. The Tuesday night group was talking about Gethsemane. Jesus' prayerful struggle before He is killed is bracketed by the story of Judas, beginning with him selling Jesus out to the chief priests for 30 pieces of silver and ending with Judas seized with remorse, trying to undo what he did, and, when he fails, killing himself.

What was decided by the group gathered in my living room is that you didn't need to be a theologian to see the story wasn't just about Judas turning his back on Jesus. The whole story is about betrayal. As we read Matthew 26 together on a dark February night, we noticed that Judas is not seen in any kind of sympathetic light. One group member said, "It seems like we have done a lot to demonize Judas. Maybe because we need a bad guy?" We read on, and discovered that between the bookends of Judas's story is the story of Peter, promising to never deny his Lord, only to do so not once but three times. And right in the middle of *that* story is this verse: "Then all the disciples deserted him [Jesus] and fled" (v. 56). Someone else said, "Wow, this is a bad day for mankind!" As the themes of manipulation, denial, and broken promises kept appearing, we began to see

///
And when I am alone, Jesus meets me in that place. He is already there in my Gethsemane waiting for me.
**

the humanness of Judas. He committed the sin of taking matters into his own hands, yes. But he was hardly alone. The author seemed to want us to see that this was not just a Judas problem. Everyone gets involved in the betrayal — us, too. Honestly, this was comforting on some level.

Together, we asked if the story is more about Jesus or the disappointing actions of the disciples. I distinctly remember our friend Sheila who spoke up and reminded us that in the middle of the disciples' betrayal, Jesus was in the garden, praying three times, and asking God if things could be different. He did this three times, just like Peter's denial. You get the impression that Jesus doesn't want the story to end this way any more than Judas or Peter or the rest of the deserters. But something about the way Jesus speaks to His friends and leans into His calling moved all of us. One of my amazing young friends, Ellrol, was quick to point out that Jesus in the garden reminded him of Dr. King as both declared a dream and a vision of a Promised Land that might be unreachable for some and misunderstood by many. I watched the faces around the room become serious as everyone quieted. This is what it means to be called to lead and to love, and it's hard. Your friends will let you down. Some might not go with you. Many won't even understand. Jesus runs back to His friends and pleads, "Stay here and keep watch with me" (v. 38). But they won't, or they can't. Then Jesus returns to His call with more clarity than ever before, relinquishing His will and His hope for companions, yet accuses and resents none of them.

No one in the room wanted to compare themselves to Dr. King, let alone Jesus. But, together we saw how the story says a lot about the lonely place of leading, about the path that Jesus walks and His invitation to follow. Ellrol kindly relieved the tension with a strangely comforting observation: "Well, I see some good news in the story. If this is the bar for being a follower of Jesus, I fit right in!" We understood what he meant. We had all found ourselves in each character in the story. If disappointment, denial, and despair were qualifications for the first disciples, none of us sitting there that Tuesday night were disqualified.

The good news is that on a day that was a bad one for being human, Jesus goes ahead of us, prays alone, calls His betrayer His friend, and walks toward the Cross. Another young person in the room said, "If I am going to lead, people aren't going to go to bat for me. Heck, they might not even go with me. And when I am alone, Jesus meets me in that place. He is already there in my Gethsemane waiting for me." This thought was captivating and lonely and comforting. Yes. We saw ourselves with Jesus being invited as leaders into a very lonely place, to walk away from power and life as we understand it and toward new life — into places that look as though they are full of shame.

This Gethsemane story seems to be a critical juncture in the way of Jesus, reminding all of us that walking with Jesus leads to places where most people have an aversion to going. The grace is that we see ourselves in all the characters. The call is to follow Jesus into this place and all that comes after it. The comfort is that when we follow, we do find Jesus there in the garden. The garden of Gethsemane is the place where Jesus is portrayed as walking alone, praying alone, and struggling with self-sacrifice. As I think about the real peacemakers in our history, people like Mother Theresa or Dr. King, this garden narrative seems to be woven through the fabric of their lives. For the one who chooses to walk the path of justice and mercy in the world and for the world, the journey leads through Gethsemane. The lesson unfolding here is that if we walk closer to the edge, we might lose friends and partners, landing in places where — like others who have entered the garden before us — Jesus is our only comfort and companion.

What the Tuesday group began to detect in Gethsemane is further illuminated in what many call the climax to Mark's Gospel. In Mark 8, we see Jesus asking His followers to follow Him into this counterintuitive journey.

> *Then he called the crowd to him along with his disciples and said: "Whoever wants to be my disciple must deny themselves and take up their cross and follow me. For whoever wants to save their life will lose it, but whoever loses their life for me and for the gospel will save it."*
>
> — MARK 8:34–35

This is Jesus' clarifying comment about His mission. Peter has rejected the idea that Jesus will be killed, and Jesus has to explain to Peter what it means to follow Him. In doing so, He invites all of us who call ourselves Christians into a paradoxical relationship between winning and losing, holding on and letting go, death and life.

VICTORY THAT LOOKS A LOT LIKE DEFEAT

My sweet little nephews, Matt and Josh, are guilty of nothing. Well, as their uncle, this is my opinion. They are only guilty of finding joy in their old ornery Uncle Ron. They both love sports and all the swag that accompanies their fanaticism. Their passion means they wear their team colors, publically declaring their allegiance. Recently, on a family vacation, I was struck by one of Matt's shirts. "I am victory," it proclaimed, alongside a shoe logo we have all grown accustomed to connecting with champions. This is all fine and good. I myself am a Seattle sports fanatic. Everyone who knows me knows my allegiance to the Seahawks and the Mariners, Husky football and basketball, and the dream that an NBA team will return to Seattle. But if I am really honest with myself, maybe this matters so much to me because it really doesn't matter at all. There, I said it. In a world in which there is so much to be concerned about, so much that matters, it's fun to care about something that doesn't really matter at all.

As I reflect on T-shirts that claim "I am victory" and allegiance to sports teams whose championships bring communities together, I think of this invitation of Jesus. Jesus declares that one finds life in denying life. Victory is in the shape of a cross. The Cross begins to expose power and proclaim how counterintuitive following Jesus is to those of us who think winners win and losers, well—we know what happens to losers. I am convinced that too much of our theology, as Western evangelicals, is imbedded in victory. The message on my nephew's shirt matches the messages of most church reader boards. They all seem to be about living victoriously, about triumph. There is good reason for this. If people feel like church gives them a chance to be a winner, attendance and commitment increase. I have never seen a church reader board proclaiming that love doesn't result in victory and that instead invites the community to follow Jesus in the way of the Cross.

> *But we preach Christ crucified: a stumbling block to Jews and foolishness to Gentiles.*
>
> —1 CORINTHIANS 1:23

The Apostle Paul claims the Cross is a stumbling block, and understands that the invitation makes little sense. The cross, the symbol of Roman political dominance, is now the Christian sign of hope. People who died on crosses were criminals and revolutionaries that Rome wanted to show who was boss. No king displays his power by being killed by a competing empire. On the face of things, the Cross shows that Jesus' revolution has failed. No wonder Paul says the idea of the Cross is hard to swallow, or just ridiculous. Yet we are asked to follow the same ridiculous path.

A THEOLOGY OF THE CROSS: NOT A NEW IDEA

During the Protestant Reformation, one of Martin Luther's critiques of the institutional church, and its unhealthy and damaging relationship with the state, was its theology of triumph. (Maybe they had too many "I am victory" T-shirts.) It was a theology he saw as not only power-driven but dishonest, an inaccurate understanding of the way of Jesus and those who follow Him. This theology of triumph had created a church rooted in ideals and expectations based on power and privilege. It caused the church to lose its moral compass. The history Luther was born into was one of crusades, colonialism, and slavery—horrible acts in the name of God. The church felt entitled to force its will on the world. Luther condemned this behavior for its basis in a theology that calls evil good and good evil, a theology that aligns the church with power and victory while missing the invitation of Christ. One could say this kind of theology jumps too quickly into the Resurrection and ignores that the pathway to get there is through death on a cross. Luther believed that for the mission of God to be revealed in the world, the church must adopt a theology rooted in an experience of the Cross.[1]

For Luther, the theology of the Cross is a journey of spiritual formation. It exposes the scandalous nature of power and privilege in the world, and invites followers of Jesus to live out the example of Christ's love, exemplified in weakness, in life hidden in death. German theologian Jürgen Moltmann claims that while Christians wouldn't outright deny the theology of the Cross, it hasn't been very popular in practice.

What I believe Luther and Moltmann are getting at is that the Cross is not simply about salvation but also represents a missional call that we as followers are called to embody as a community. The question I ask myself is, how do we become a Cross-shaped people who more effectively communicate the story of Jesus to the world in a way that brings about the justice of God's kingdom?

The Cross exposes things about life, death, and power that are otherworldly, mysterious, and disorientating. The Cross is about redemption, yes. But in Mark 8, we are invited to take a journey in which losing our life actually gives life, and hanging on to life actually suffocates it. Life for the Christian is shaped by a sacrificial love for the world and a way of being that exposes the powers of this world as null and void.

This could be why missiologist Lesslie Newbigin calls the Cross of Jesus the final act and the final parable of Jesus' human life. *Parable*, meaning the acting out or telling of a story that invites us, the audience, into experiencing or acting out the same story. The question is, what is this acting out, and how does it display an alternative to the kingdom of this world?

JESUS ASKS HIS DISCIPLES TO FOLLOW

Jesus and his disciples went on to the villages around Caesarea Philippi. On the way he asked them, "Who do people say I am?" They replied, "Some say John the Baptist; others say Elijah; and still others, one of the prophets." "But what about you?" he asked. "Who do you say I am?" Peter answered, "You are the Messiah." Jesus warned them not to tell anyone about him. He then began to teach them that the Son of Man must suffer many things and be rejected by the elders, the chief priests and the teachers of the law, and that he must be killed and after three days rise again. He spoke plainly about this, and Peter took him aside and began to rebuke him. But when Jesus turned and looked at his disciples, he rebuked Peter. "Get behind me, Satan!" he said. "You do not have in mind the concerns of God, but merely human concerns." Then he called the crowd to him along with his disciples and said: "Whoever wants to be my disciple must deny themselves and take up their cross and follow me. For whoever wants to save their life will lose it, but whoever loses their life for me and for the gospel will save it."

—MARK 8:27–35

The good news of Mark's Gospel is that we have the opportunity to learn from the disciples' flawed — or should I say *bad* — example. Remember, if disappointment, denial, and despair didn't disqualify them, it shouldn't disqualify us. So far in Mark's story, we have seen a water-walking, demon-cleansing, crowd-feeding Son of God who tells most everyone not to reveal His deeds. Jesus is the Deliverer, the Messiah, but One who is veiled in secrecy. Even His own disciples expected a far different savior. No one would believe Jesus' mission, even if He told them. This is what scholars call the messianic secret. But here in the Book of Mark, sitting right in the middle of 16 chapters, is the climax of the story. Jesus asks His disciples who people are saying He is and what they think about His mission. Then He asks them who *they* think He is. Peter answers, and his answer is right on. But as one of my Pepperdine theology professors used to tell us, small theological boats should stay close to shore. Peter should quit while he is ahead. Jesus begins to elaborate on Peter's answer, and Peter quickly corrects Him, earning sharp words from Jesus. But the story doesn't end there. It ends with an invitation. You can't follow Jesus by doing anything less than losing your life. Jesus is saying that through weakness, powerlessness, and death grow victory, strength, and life. That what might look nonsensical or like a stumbling block or scandal actually holds the key to being a follower of Jesus and being part of transforming the world we live in.

///

The smell ran through the halls like air conditioning vented through the building.

We rushed to a local hospital in a large city in Kenya. My friend Dan had befriended many of the street boys in Katali, and I was traveling through Kenya with his organization, Until Then, talking to local pastors about serving and loving these boys. Dan had gotten word that one of the Katali boys he was very close to, John, had died in the street, and he hoped to get to the hospital before they disposed of the body. It was unclear what had happened, but the boy's street friends had found him in the road, passed out, and were unable to revive him. He was gone, they told Dan on a brief and static-filled phone call. We traveled from Kisumu, a long drive of three or four hours if the roads were good. (I have learned in my few trips to Kenya, you don't gauge distance in miles, but by access. Good roads, short travel. Bad roads, who knows?)

As we drove, Dan began to reflect on his friend. John had been about eighteen years old, and was a miracle, really. A lot of kids don't make it that long. Life on the streets in a big city in Africa is tough. Most street kids inhale solvent (paint or glue), a cheap lethal drug that suppresses appetite and keeps you warm and somewhat sedated, but in the long term destroys your liver and eats up brain cells. Who knows what had caused John to collapse — maybe his liver had failed, maybe he had been assaulted. The other street boys could only guess. All they knew was that he was gone, and they didn't know what to do next.

A few hours and a hundred bumpy miles later the phone rang again. It was one of the boys. "He is alive!" they proclaimed. Dan could get no clarifying information. Was he raised from the dead? In

Africa, many of our colleagues believed this to be a real possibility. Was he conscious? All we knew was that the boys would meet us at the local public hospital in Kitali.

I had no idea what I was about to encounter. Our destination was a hospital willing to receive street boys in an area with no public health care and no insurance for anyone. Dan cautioned me that the hospital would be a sad one at best.

We rolled into a gravel parking lot bordered by a small strip of grass and a snack shack. People, old and young, in all states of ill health, huddled in small patches of shade. This was the waiting room, I discovered. What these patients were waiting for was never made clear. Neither was how long they would have to wait. They just sat there, quiet, patient, and, for the most part, expressionless.

I walked into a "hospital" that smelled like an open sore. I am sure that the few doctors and medical staff there were doing the best with all they had, and were forced every day to make medical decisions I hope I never have to make. But I must say my first and strongest impression was the smell. I could feel it in my forehead and in my mouth, and I knew it was the manifestation of open, infected wounds. The smell ran through the halls like air conditioning vented through the building. We walked past very sick people, who lay on soiled mattresses, surrounded by family and covered with worn blankets.

///

They understood, intuitively, not to ignore the impulse to care for another out of self-preservation.

**

John lay sleeping, or maybe unconscious, at the end of the long hall. He was unclothed, his midsection covered by a sheet. No family stood around him, just three street boys. One appeared to be cleaning a mess underneath him; another was smashing a banana to feed to him. A third boy approached us and gave Dan a handshake that is somehow universal among young men on the streets around the world. A handshake that confirmed that Dan was the father or brother they had

///
The power of this world is exposed, and life is found in death. Death to illusions of power, death to systems of oppression, and life found in letting go.
**

always wanted. I felt a wave of guilt for hoping that I would escape this place without touching anything.

The story of John's rising from the dead was now illuminated by the street boy. John had been brought to the hospital and pronounced dead upon his arrival. Then he had been dragged to the hospital morgue and stacked in a pile of dead bodies. Somehow, as the doctor or intern assigned to the morgue began to sort out what was next for all these corpses, he noticed a slight movement in John's chest. He checked for a heart rate and, upon discovering John was not dead, brought him back to the land of the living. Living, but still dangerously ill with meningitis or something worse. The "something worse" seemed like a real possibility here. There was no clean bedding, no real equipment, no privacy, and what appeared to be little sanitation. If you didn't have an opportunistic infection when you arrived, it seemed like there was a good chance of taking one home with you. If you got out alive.

As the story became clear, I also saw more plainly what the boys were doing for their friend. They were cleaning up a bowel movement and preparing his meal, which they had gotten from a few other street boys. A doctor stopped by and told us, the two white men, what medicine was needed and where we could buy it. The boys said they would sit with John so the food, sheet, and clean drinking water didn't end up with someone else. As we walked away from John's bed, Dan looked at me and asked, "How many pastors would do that for a street boy?" The last thing I had seen was one of the boys gently taking the mashed banana and placing it in John's mouth.

This is the message of the Cross — great power concealed in weakness. Boys willing to take the last of what they had to give to a friend. Children who had to get their own needs met by any means possible in order to survive, suspending their needs for a friend struggling to stay alive. "Greater love has no one than this: to lay down one's life for one's friends" (John 15:13).

In that moment I watched these boys lose themselves for the sake of another. They understood, intuitively, not to ignore the impulse to care for another out of self-preservation. I have seen this a thousand times with kids on the streets everywhere — they sense that the impulse to give life away is the only real way to save it.

The other thing I witnessed in that poor Kenyan hospital ward was a radical form of truth telling. This hospital declared in some pretty ugly ways that we live in a world where some get medical attention and some don't. A chart with John's medical status was jammed into the footboard of his bed. Next to "Name" were the words "street boy." John's friends stood together in radical defiance of this label as they washed the body of a boy made in the likeness of God. In these boys' love and care, they held court, putting on trial all the powers that ignored and dismissed him. In their witness of love in weakness, the powers of this world were for a moment exposed for the façade they are, and the power of the self-giving love of true friends dying to their own needs was revealed.

Let's be honest. When Paul uses the Cross as one of his most significant metaphors, his audience knows what he means: death. The cross was for criminals and zealots. The very public and shameful act proclaimed: "Don't you dare mess with Rome." Paul gets that Jesus made what was considered sure defeat and turned it into victory. The power of Rome is disarmed, and what looks weak and deadly somehow leads to life. Rome and the power of this world is exposed, and life is found in death. Death to illusions of power, death to systems of oppression, and life found in letting go.

Fredrick Buechner observes:

> When Jesus says that whoever would save his life will lose it and whoever loses his life will save it, surely he is not making a statement about how, morally speaking, life *ought* to be. Rather, he is making a statement about how life *is*.

The truth is, the tighter we hold on to life, the more we strangle it, and, paradoxically, the more it slips through our fingers. But the more we are willing to let go, the more we discover life. We are literally invited to lose our lives. As Paul says in the Book of Philippians, "to live is Christ and to die is gain" (1:21). But we have to take the risk in order to find out whether this is true, whether, in Buechner's words, this is how life is. Can we trust what Jesus is saying and let go and die?

Let me clarify. Self-denial can often end up taking a form of self-negation that leads to a kind of passive-aggressiveness and codependency. Codependency is a system of homeostatic behavior — an attempt to keep things in balance by overlooking what is really happening — that manifests in a broken or unhealthy family or community in order to avoid disrupting the status quo. It staves off a crisis that could lead to important change by suppressing the true desires of individuals who are in relationship with each other. But if the way of the Cross is about how self-denial exposes the powers that be for what they are, then I don't believe that dying to self is about codependency. The Cross asks individuals to lose their lives in a much different way. It demands that we all enter into the vulnerable space of declaring what really is — and there is a lot of risk in doing this — rather than clinging to how we hope things are. In a broken system, this truth-telling feels like death, but it is the only chance of gaining new or resurrected life.

The Cross is not the way of self-deprecation. It doesn't tell us that we deserve nothing good and beat down the human heart as unlovable or unworthy. But it does ask us to be honest about where real life is found, and where artificial life has been manufactured as a coping mechanism to distract

///
The Cross could mean denying the American dream and exposing the lie of materialism, exposing systems that hoard power and oppress others.
**

us from finding that real life. Here's what I think happens: we don't really believe we deserve or understand how to find the good, so we hedge our bets and attach ourselves to the "good enough." The Cross exposes this covert despair. It asks us to die to the safety we hold on to. When Jesus tells us to pick up our crosses, we are denying, not the self God created us to be, but the self that falls victim to athletic shoe commercials and visions of authority that promise us triumph. The public spectacle of Christ crucified tells the truth about the uselessness of power and invites us to live out the same truth as we take up our own crosses and follow Him.

Jesus invites all of us into a new way of being human. For some this could mean telling the truth in a codependent system where equilibrium is maintained through damaging self-denial. To be honest about your needs — a much harder and healthier way to live. For others the Cross could mean denying the American dream and exposing the lie of materialism, exposing systems that hoard power and oppress others the way Rome did. The spiritual journey of the Cross means illuminating the truth, letting go of illusions, seeing things the way they really are, and being willing to forgive.

///
This kind of vulnerable love is a crazy tightrope-walking love.
**

In exposing the powers of this world, Jesus not only journeys to the most shame-filled place in our world to die a criminal's death — He blames and accuses no one. We, too, are called to this place where no record of wrongs is kept and where we can resist the urge to make villains out of our enemies.

The Cross, then, is a grace to us. A bad day for being human becomes the first day of a new created order. The Cross invites us to live in the world by dying to illusions that don't really sustain us and to self in its most narcissistic form. Mark 8 is an invitation for us to make space in our lives, to refuse the emptiness of power, and trust that the way of Jesus is the way to truth-telling and real life. But it can be a lonely place. The disciples fled from this lonely place more than once, and so do we. But we are always invited back in, to learn from Jesus how to save our lives by letting them go — to make space for others through our own death and entrance into relationship, with Jesus and the world He loves. This is where the power of God lies: letting go of our hoped-for outcomes and sitting in the space of powerlessness with and for the world.

Modeling this letting go is the only way to shake ourselves loose of the natural urgency we feel to save our own lives. This kind of vulnerable love is a crazy tightrope-walking love that must have full assurance in the One who sends us out to invite the world to come with us on the journey—to let go of the illusions of life for real life itself.

Can we choose this way of the Cross and faithfully believe that it is in death that we and others are set free? Not with our great doctrines, not with our spotless image but by dying to the images of power that hold us captive. Dying to the life we hold on to that is so much less than the life we were created to live. Risking our lives on Jesus' promise that this is the only way we will find true life.

CHAPTER 8

WHERE ARE YOU WILLING TO GO?

Very truly I tell you, when you were younger you dressed yourself and went where you wanted; but when you are old you will stretch out your hands, and someone else will dress you and lead you where you do not want to go.

—JOHN 21:18

If you follow Jesus, the question is really, what do you expect? And where are you willing to go? Truth be told, most of us want more control than life allows. But as we love the world, try to do justice, and enter into the world's suffering, we find ourselves on the threshold of the unfamiliar, in places of little or no control, and we ask others to step into the unknown, the barely perceivable space that is at the very least disorienting. Of course all of us have hopes and dreams of the way life is supposed to be. But often suffering and disappointment land in a spot between the real and ideal, between what we think life ought to be and what life really is. I believe this is why many of us have such a hard time navigating the suffering in the world. We have so denied our own suffering, masked our own fears, and stuffed down our own disappointment that to even consider entering into the experience of another's suffering in a meaningful way — whether or not that suffering looks like our own — might mean having to come to grips with the sadness and tragedy we feel in our own lives. We struggle to make sense of this suffering, disappointment, and unrealized expectations. It makes the ideas of a loving God and good people experiencing such difficulty hard to hold at the same time. Sometimes we create a God in our own image that matches our hopes and dreams.

Philosopher Peter Rollins addresses this issue in books like *How (Not) To Speak of God* and *The Idolatry of God,* claiming that those of us who live in the postmodern Western world have created a god who is what we want and need in order to pacify our own frustration and disappointment. We Westerners have a hard time letting go of that ideal to take a sober look at what actually is. I think for many of us our own expectations of God and how we want life to be have become the ideal, and that's difficult to relinquish. This is the great tragedy of making an image of God where nothing bad happens; we may miss seeing where God is in the midst of circumstances that don't meet our expectations.

So, where is God in our own and others' suffering, disappointment, and unmet expectations? How do we live trying to do justice when we suffer and others suffer around us?

In 2009, after serving in an incredible place, New Horizons, and loving incredible kids for 27 years, I felt this nudging, this tugging. I was completing my first book, and Linda was launching a new business. It was time for us to move on, but to what and where, I did not have a clue.[1] For the next five years, I traveled a lot, teaching in amazing places, and Linda worked long hours in a cafe, called Street Bean, she had started as an offshoot of New Horizons, to employ young people from the program. We both worked hard, money was tight, and we wondered if our work together, really together, had come to an end. We had been working side by side in ministry since before our marriage. I finished the book and Linda successfully got the coffee shop up and running. I helped Linda at the shop, she was the first reader on every new chapter of my first book, we supported each other, but our work was different. These five years were productive, but mostly, I felt like I waited, wondered, and wandered. I felt lost, my identity shaken and my future vague, I was terrified and unsure of what was next.

I was forty-seven years old when I left New Horizons, the only job I had had since my twenty-second birthday. This was the place where Linda and I had met, married,

///
[John's] endorsement comes from the lame, blind, deaf, poor, and dead folk who have no vote!
**

raised our children, and grown up ourselves, where we learned our theology and learned how to love. At the end of my time there, I walked to beautiful Myrtle Edwards Park, one of the urban parks that borders Puget Sound, and tossed my building key toward the Olympic mountain range. It made it about 50 feet from shore and sounded no different than a small rock hitting a fairly large puddle. But this was symbolic. It was a building key with *#1* engraved on the side, the first key issued to the New Horizons drop-in center that I helped open, that I had helped raise $1.5 million to purchase and renovate — a small electric plant transformed into a safe space for street kids. My own kids had birthday parties there on nights the center was closed. This was the place I had eaten 27 Thanksgiving dinners and wrapped Christmas gifts 27 times. This was the place where we had entered into life together with vulnerable kids. On this day I tossed my access to this past and a huge part of my identity into the Sound and hoped to embrace the future. Linda was cultivating a wonderful work environment for kids exiting street life, and I was going to teach the next generation of ministry practitioners. It was the start of a new chapter. I traveled, taught, and preached at amazing churches. But most of the time I felt alone, without a business card that clarified my position and the place I came from, and no idea how I was going to get paid.

The café grew and Linda put her soul in this beautiful place where community, justice, and beauty danced among former street kids and the business people they were serving in the Belltown neighborhood. Linda had stood with me through multiple academic programs; it was my turn to stand with her. She ran Street Bean, and I hung out there, writing, talking with customers, organizing the art and music. And I wondered what was next for me, with Linda still partnering with New Horizons. I felt trapped in the past. I struggled, and she graciously heard me in my frustration — mostly frustration with myself. Some days I actually enjoyed — at some level — what was being revealed in me.

I traveled to Guatemala to teach at Setteca, a seminary in Guatemala City. On this trip, Linda and I were able to travel to the mountains and meet the families who were growing the coffee for Street Bean. We showed them pictures of the café, and realized that somehow the miracle of Guatemalan farmers and street kids in Seattle using coffee to reclaim and sustain their lives was actually happening. Then Linda began to feel the same nudging that I had felt two years prior. She had been the nursemaid to this miraculous business. She had poured herself out for this place and the young people working there, and now it was time to pass it on to the next generation of leaders. Linda found her replacement, served alongside him, taught him all she knew, celebrated the unique gifts he could bring, then let go. She, too, stepped out into nothing. So we wandered and we wondered together. Some days, life was sustained by daily bread. Other days we felt like we were just treading water. We were both closing in on fifty and had no idea where we were going. This waiting was lasting way too long.

NOTHING NEW: EXPECTATION AND DISAPPOINTMENT

After Jesus had finished instructing his twelve disciples, he went on from there to teach and preach in the towns of Galilee. When John, who was in prison, heard about the deeds of the Messiah, he sent his disciples to ask him, "Are you the one who is to come, or should we expect someone else?" Jesus replied, "Go back and report to John what you hear and see: The blind receive sight, the lame walk, those who have leprosy are cleansed, the deaf hear, the dead are raised, and the good news is proclaimed to the poor."

—MATTHEW 11:1–5

Let's remember who John is in this text: a street prophet from the desert. He is not endorsed by the powers that be; he has no religious clout, royal office, or temple credentials. He is one of the same people who Jesus has been walking with and is talking about here. His endorsement comes from the lame, blind, deaf, poor, and dead folk who have no vote! He has been baptizing for the forgiveness of sins. In doing so, according to N. T. Wright, he is saying to all

///

Blessed is anyone who is not disappointed in me.

\\\

these lame, blind folk, what you thought was available only to a few through the temple can now happen anywhere and is for anyone through the ministry of John. But John not only announces a temple alternative — he proclaims that the kingdom of heaven has come near in his cousin Jesus. He announces this new kingdom is right here, setting up camp in the middle of all of us. In the Gospel of John, he makes a huge declaration that Jesus is the Lamb of God who takes away the sins of the world (John 1:29).

Now, this man who has ushered in the Lord, who has proclaimed that freedom and deliverance have come, sits in prison. He is a captive. His future is in question, and what he has preached, he might never see come to pass. Something has gone terribly wrong for John. The text says that when John heard what Jesus was doing, something about it is confusing to him. He takes issue with something about the way Jesus was acting out this new kingdom John had proclaimed. So John sends his disciples for clarification. Jesus begins to explain, and in this moment we see John's disappointment. It's not that there isn't freedom and deliverance. It is that John is not experiencing those things — not like he expected. He is sitting in jail. This isn't working out like he had planned.

John is not the only one guilty of confusing expectations with reality. Later in the text, the unbelieving towns Jesus has performed miracles in stand accused. He calls them more ignorant than Sodom and Gomorrah, and says that if those two cities had seen what these towns have seen in John and Jesus, they would still be standing. The crowd is guilty as well. Jesus points out that John came to them as an ascetic (someone we might call puritanical today), and they said he had a demon, and now Jesus comes with feasting, and is called a glutton and drunkard (Matthew 11:19). The towns and the crowds all seem to think they know what they are looking for, and Jesus needs to clarify a few things. Matthew 11:6 seems to be the crux of all the confusion over what this Jesus is really all about: "Blessed is anyone who does not stumble on account of me." In my opinion, a better translation is, "Blessed is anyone *who is not disappointed in me.*" John, the crowds, and the towns all seem to share in their disappointment in Jesus.

///

In the middle of that long stretch of time between jobs, when things were not working out like I had planned, I was in some way comforted by Jesus' cousin, John. Some commentators have suggested that Jesus could have been with John and his disciples for a long period of time before Jesus' baptism and John's declaration of Jesus' role and identity. Imagine for a minute John with his group of revolutionaries, sitting around dreaming of change. Making radical commitments for the sake of this vision, eating a simple diet of bugs and honey, wearing simple clothes, separating themselves in hopes of the kingdom they keep praying will come. And then as they sit and talk with John's cousin, his playmate since he and Jesus were little, John begins to see something in Him. He begins to imagine that the stories his mother has told him might be true. Now it is Jesus' time,

///

Go see what Jesus is doing, because what He's doing and what I hoped for aren't lining up.

\\\

and John is thrilled because all he has gambled on seems worth it. What he had hoped for is materializing in his cousin, right here right now. But right when this thing really gets going, John is arrested and put in jail. And John does what we all do — ask your friends to find the guy you endorsed and get an explanation. Because a Roman jail doesn't seem like the outcome you imagined.

What was revealed to me about myself during this long period of waiting is that I was really not disappointed with God as much as I was with all of my expectations of what I had hoped God would be or would do. Many of my own prayers as I moved into what felt so unfamiliar were similar to John's request of his friends: *go see what Jesus is doing, because what He's doing and what I hoped for aren't lining up.* In the voice of John, I hear my own disappointment. I left all that was familiar and comfortable. I was told that God had my back, but then in the middle of waiting, I wondered if I had been wrong to step out.

Now I want you to know, during this time, it appeared like things were OK, even moving on a steady trajectory. I published a book and taught on three continents. We launched a theological roundtable for young leaders in our community, the Tuesday night group. But we were also wondering how we were going to pay our bills. We longed to know where we were going and with whom we were going to serve. Even in the midst of all the good things that were happening, we had no idea where we were going next. We were drifting down a river, knowing it was ridiculous to even try to grab the wet rocks that masqueraded as stability. So we just floated and bobbed, drifting with the current.

As I lived in what felt like John's utter confusion and disappointment, I kept hearing the echoes of a far more ancient passage.

A passage so scandalous, that after Genesis 22, it is never mentioned again in Hebrew Scripture. It is the Binding of Isaac. Daily I walked into the wilderness, and as I did, the walk Abraham made up the side of a mountain kept dropping into my mind. The story goes something like this: Abraham is asked by God to give up his son, to take him up a mountain, bind him, and sacrifice him to God. The very son that is the child of promise. The future Abraham has been promised is now to be given back. Abraham is obedient to what he thinks God has told him, and as he walks up the mountain with his son, Isaac asks a question, pointing out the obvious fact that they have no animal to sacrifice. Abraham reassures Isaac that God will provide. The end of the story seems to end all right. Abraham's hand is stayed by the angel of the Lord, and a ram is provided as an alternative to killing his own son.[2] I have heard from many of my Jewish friends who walk to synagogue past my house that the Jewish community would never call this the sacrifice of Isaac. *Binding*, or *the offering*, yes, but never *the sacrifice*. In the text, God does not seem to have ever intended Abraham to actually kill Isaac. This killing of a child is too terrible to consider.

WHERE DO THESE STORIES MERGE?

John sits in a prison cell and Abraham walks up a hill. John's future and the seed of Abraham are both in doubt. What they both believed is suddenly in question. If it isn't God's intention to ask Abraham to kill his son, maybe he is being asked to offer his future, exemplified in the life of Isaac. This same future that God promised, God is now asking to be offered back. Both Abraham and John ask the same questions that we all ask when our future is in doubt and our own expectations seem to be disintegrating: *God, are You good? Are You sure that those who trust in You are never really put to shame?*

I'll tell you what, in the middle of Linda and me not having "jobs" and living on income from whatever adjunct class I was teaching, sermon I was preaching, or the generous gift from someone in our community, I felt shame, and a lot of it. I found myself trying to explain what we were waiting for, planning for. And I think I got the same looks Noah did when he told folks he was building a big boat in a place where it never rained.

But this is the power of the story of Abraham and Isaac. As I read through it, I have noticed something very interesting about how Abraham refers to God. He uses two very different names in the text. On the way up the mountain (Genesis 22:1, 3, 8, 9, 12), he uses the word *Elohim*, the generic name for God — a formal title but in no way a personal name describing God as a participant in the human story. But after Abraham has laid his future on the altar, the future promised by God, a new name emerges in the text (Genesis 22:11, 14, 15, 16): *Yahweh* or *Lord*. The God of Moses, who will be what He will be, no matter what you expect. A God who will define God's self.

There is indeed a test of faith here. Abraham's future is in doubt. But it is unclear who or what is being tested: Abraham or Elohim — Abraham's idea of God. The ultimate test. Will we be able to let go of Elohim to see God as Yahweh? But maybe Yahweh won't be the God Abraham, John, or I expected or imagined. I don't want to paint the end of the story too positively. For Abraham there is a ram in the bushes. But for John, all that awaits him is a beheading. Another

///

My problem wasn't with God, but with my expectations of God that were driving my own ideal.

****

happy ending to a Bible story we don't much talk about. It's like preaching on the text from the psalm about dashing your enemy neighbors' kids against the rocks, or on the passage in Lamentations where Daughter Zion is desperate enough to consider killing her own child in order to eat and survive one more day.

///

In the five years that I sat in the land of the in-between, I learned something. I realized that in many ways I had hoped for certainty and for comfort. I was taken to a place where I had to relinquish all that I thought was true, all that I had hoped for. And in this place of confusion and chaos, when my very future was in doubt, in that empty space God redefined God's self and redefined me.

John looks to Jesus and says, "What you're doing doesn't make any sense." Jesus' response is: "Blessed is he who isn't disappointed by me, by my way of doing things." Jesus' way, He goes on to say in Matthew 11:25, has been hidden from the wise, but little children, the ones who have no understanding and no expectations, to them the kingdom is revealed. The little children see it. John and me? We kinda missed it.

My problem wasn't with God, but with my expectations of God that were driving my own ideal. I needed that gap between the real and ideal to open up before me. I needed that empty, terrifyingly silent space to examine my own unmet hopes and dreams. It was during this time that I had to evaluate why and how I would proceed. I had to let go and truly move on. I tell my students that it took no time at all for the children of Israel to get out of Egypt, but it took 40 years to get Egypt out of the children of Israel. I needed the same thing. It was hard. I wanted to run back to comfort, to security, to what was familiar. I wanted to create a familiar image that would comfort me.

I was not accustomed to God being so silent for so long, and in this silence, with the future completely unknown, I was being exposed as me. This is the part of walking with Jesus that is so hard to embrace — a

///

So, for the world's sake, are we willing to give up what we imagined for something that might be far different — and better — than we had hoped?

\\\

walking in silence, with an unknown outcome that I find teaches me about the devils and fears in my own heart.

I have begun to believe that right in the middle of what might seem like dead ends and disappointments, God creates something new. When my idea of my future and, to a large degree, my very idea of God is utterly dashed, it makes room for new possibilities and for new images of God that my own limited construct would not allow. So, for the world's sake, are we willing to give up what we imagined for something that might be far different — and better — than we had hoped? Are we willing to let our future go, to let it remain open and undefined? Some of us will, like Abraham, get to a place where we are given a fresh experience of and name for God. Others of us will be like John, finding ourselves renamed through the journey. Jesus calls John *Elijah*, the great prophet of the ancient Hebrews, who calls out the prophets of Baal to bring fire from heaven, Elijah who is comforted by the still small voice of God. John, the courageous voice who comes in the spirit of the great Hebrew prophet, will be comforted. But for all of us, this experience of confusion and disorientation will mean letting go of what we *thought* was true for what really *is*.

///

In his book *Reaching Out*, Henri Nouwen says that the spiritual journey is always a movement from the familiar to the unknown. Moving from hostility to hospitality, illusion to prayer, and from loneliness to solitude. If I am asking others to jump into the unknown, I always ask myself how willing I am to do the same. In my own faith tradition, I have heard it preached from the pulpit often: "You can't take no one where you ain't willing to go." So when it comes to the work of justice, the question here is: Are we willing to step into the unfamiliar and the unknown as an act of faith and spiritual formation, recognizing that this is what we are asking the people we are forming relationships with to do? Every time we encourage a homeless man to think about entering a housing program, or a woman caught in a cycle of domestic abuse to leave and go to a shelter, or an adolescent who is drug addicted to go to treatment, we are asking them to take this spiritual step from the familiar to the unknown. My encouragement is simply this: Can we, too, move toward the unknown, modeling to the world a spiritual journey that is faith-filled and far from certain? Can we honestly explore these empty spaces in our own lives? Pulling the curtain back on the places of tragedy, suffering, and disappointment will give us genuine empathy and credibility as we invite others to do the same. It is only by leaning into the hard places that we can begin to invite others to make the journey as well. You can't take no one where you ain't willing to go.

CHAPTER 9

FORGIVENESS SETS THEM, AND US, FREE

Growing up Pentecostal, I was taught that the Holy Spirit gathers with us whenever we meet together. I was also taught to expect the Spirit of God to be moving in the world, guiding, directing, and bringing spiritual gifts to life—exemplified in the "fruit" that shows up in the lives of Jesus' followers. I am grateful for the Pentecostal stream of Christian spirituality. I grew as a boy believing that God was among us. And by God's Spirit, Wisdom, as the Orthodox Church calls it, God would be reveled among us. I was taught to expect it, but in my Pentecostal tradition, I would also often hear that the evidence of being filled with this Spirit meant speaking in tongues—a heavenly language that comforts and guides the prayers of people who sit somewhere between the kingdom of this world and the kingdom of God. I have no interest in making a theological statement about this being good or bad, correct or incorrect. I do, though, want to simply point out that in John's Gospel, the sign that marked the lives of Jesus followers was forgiveness, and they were forgiven and they were sent to extend this forgiveness to the world:

> *And with that he breathed on them and said, "Receive the Holy Spirit. If you forgive anyone's sins, their sins are forgiven; if you do not forgive them, they are not forgiven."*
>
> —JOHN 20:22–23

In John's Gospel, Jesus enters the locked room in His resurrected form and breathes on His disciples. The wind, or breath, metaphor for the Spirit of the Almighty entering into human experience is a predominate image throughout Scripture. The Hebrew word for *Spirit* as wind or breath shows up often in the Old Testament. It is the breath that gives life to creation and strength to the prophets, it is a sign of God's presence in the Book of Psalms, and it is the image used in Acts when the breath of God appears to the disciples in the upper room, empowering them to be sent out in forgiveness.

In the middle of Matthew's Gospel, Jesus gives a sermon. It seems to be a very important sermon and occupies much of Matthew's narrative. Amidst this sermon — one of the longest sections of teaching in any Gospel — sits a prayer, the Lord's Prayer. And at the end of the prayer, Jesus offers a strong word about forgiveness — in the same manner that you forgive, you will be forgiven.

I do not believe the implication here is that God's forgiveness is dependent on our ability to forgive. But these verses do seem to call attention to our posture in the world and how that affects our reality. I strongly believe that if we do not do the hard work of forgiveness, the cancer of unforgiveness will so permeate our existence, we will not have the power or freedom to live as forgiven people. An inability to forgive does ugly work in all of us. I believe we should be people that give and request forgiveness freely. To give and ask for forgiveness is a crucial step in reconciling with others, and reconciliation and justice utterly depend on each other.

As mature adults, we (hopefully) see more and more the benefit of giving others this grace-filled break. As I get a bit older and look back over my life, I can acknowledge that most people who have hurt me are not as bad as I originally thought. I have grown in the realization that hurt people are the ones who hurt people, a reality far more complicated than my perception of my own pain.

> With a little time, and little more insight, we begin to see both ourselves and our enemies in humbler profiles. We are not really as innocent as we felt when we were first hurt. And we do not usually have a gigantic monster to forgive. We have a weak, needy, and somewhat stupid human being. When you see your enemy and yourself in the weakness and silliness of the humanity you share, you will make the miracle of forgiving a little easier.
>
> —LEWIS B. SMEDES

I have read this quote by ethicist Lewis Smedes for years, and it has always helped me to be able to logically look at forgiveness. It helps me come to grips with the realization that those who have wounded me are human, like me. The longer I serve alongside others, the more I realize that much of what activates me in those I am working with is in some way closely related to my own faults and shortcomings. And if I am really honest, much of what I think are malicious acts of others is really them acting out of the insecurities and fears that I too am very acquainted with.

> *///*
> *Sometimes the damage is so big that it can only be repaired through the power of forgiveness.*
> **

It is equally important to acknowledge that misuses of power, like racism, sexism, child abuse, and sexual assault, are not to be dealt with lightly. The work of justice and reconciliation demands that we don't simply forgive and forget, that we do not too quickly embrace a resolution that doesn't allow adequate time and space to sit with the severity of these wounds. Some issues are big, complex, and deeply damaging. The process of forgiveness can be long and incredibly complicated.

That being said, Desmond Tutu, bishop in the Anglican Church in South Africa, has expressed that the key to his people moving on from the horrors of apartheid in his country, simply stated is, "We forgive them." We learn from Bishop Tutu that forgiveness — not forgetting or even fixing what has been damaged — but forgiveness, hard-won and courageous, found in the midst of people telling the unvarnished stories of their pain, was key in the face of atrocities.

But the theological puzzle remains: How is our ability to forgive connected to God holding no record of wrongs? And what does it mean that the disciples can give or withhold forgiveness?

> *For if you forgive other people when they sin against you, your heavenly Father will also forgive you. But if you do not forgive others their sins, your Father will not forgive your sins.*
>
> — MATTHEW 6:14–15

So here again, at the heart of this sermon in Matthew — what we call the Sermon on the Mount — sits a prayer, the Lord's Prayer. And at the end of the prayer, Jesus offers a strong word about forgiveness — in the same manner that you forgive, you will be forgiven.

Again, I do not believe the implication here is that God's forgiveness is dependent on our ability to forgive. Forgiveness isn't saying whatever wrong you have incurred isn't a big deal. Forgiveness might be saying the exact opposite. Sometimes the damage is so big that it can only be repaired through the power of forgiveness. It might never be forgotten and it simply cannot be fixed, so in the end, it must be forgiven. Forgiveness sets me free to move on from what I hoped for and planned, believing and trusting in God for what He will do. Forgiveness holds no record of wrongs because it wells up from a source of life that isn't about keeping accounts.

Richard Rohr, in his book *Breathing Under Water,* states that "Forgiveness is to let go of our hope for a different or better past." This letting go acknowledges that there is a reality far outside human interaction. It is also the most difficult gift we can ever give to our friends, family, community, and the world. Letting go relinquishes control, but letting go might set us free. The cycle of forgiveness, asking for forgiveness, and extending forgiveness is an otherworldly way to live. It moves hope from the here and now to an otherworldly and eternal construct.

In the section of the Sermon on the Mount that precedes the Lord's Prayer in Matthew, Jesus teaches using a few "do nots" that reveal what Jesus wants His audience to learn — or possibly unlearn. Do not draw attention to yourself when you give alms. Don't pray loudly in public. Don't use so many words when you pray. And the "do nots" continue after the prayer: when you fast, don't draw attention to yourself with a sad face. Do not judge, do not worry about food or drink, and definitely do not worry about tomorrow. Jesus is teaching about true religion. Jesus in Matthew is the new lawgiver, like Moses, setting out the kingdom's ethics in this sermon on the mountain. This prayer that emphasizes forgiveness at the center of the sermon is the lynchpin of all these "do nots," the high point of this new form of spirituality. The Lord's Prayer focuses on God's sovereignty and welcoming God's way into the world. And then comes the biggest "do not": "But if you do not forgive others their sins, your Father will not forgive your sins" (Matthew 6:15).

///

Sometimes the families of the Bible make me feel like all my difficulties with my family of origin and its dysfunctions are nothing by comparison.

**

How is Rohr's comment about letting go of the past connected to Jesus'"do nots"? Consider for a minute the alternatives to forgiveness: resentment, bitterness, vengeance, judgment. As I look at Jesus'"do nots" and my own attempts to hold on to a past that I would love to reinvent or make different, I see the elements of control. I feel a sense of power when I can hold on. But forgiveness both asked for and given is the ultimate act of letting go. Fear makes me feel like I am in control, as does resentment, bitterness, vengeance, and judgment. They all come with the illusions of power and control. Forgiveness relinquishes control, and letting go of the hope that the past could be different makes room for new possibilities in the future.

THE TWO COATS OF JOSEPH

The story of Joseph is found in the later part of Genesis. Joseph is his father's favorite child. At least it appears this way. He is the baby boy. And as with many youngest children, the older siblings realize that mom and dad have mellowed, relaxed the rules, and maybe shortened the chore list. And as with so many family stories, Joseph's brothers are sick of it. Dad doesn't help much with quelling this jealousy. He makes Joseph a beautiful coat that says the person it was designed for was someone above or beyond hard labor. Joseph doesn't help his case either. (Lewis Smedes might say he is not as innocent as he thought he was.) Joseph shows up in the nice coat and tells his older, hardworking brothers that he's having dreams about his potential and how someday they will all bow to him. We can all see what's happening. A recipe for sibling rivalry. In the middle of this rivalry, resentment, and jealousy, the brothers make a plan to kill him. This is when the story gets really Old Testament. Cooler heads prevail, Joseph's death is staged, the coat is smeared with goat's blood, and Joseph is thrown in a pit and sold to some traders passing by. Sometimes the families of the Bible make me feel like all my difficulties with my family of origin and its dysfunctions are nothing by comparison.

So Joseph is sold into Egypt, and in the middle of a bad situation, he makes the best of it, serving a military official and gaining status. That is until the good-looking Joseph is pursued by the military official's wife. This time he doesn't take the time to brag about his wardrobe. In fact, he runs right out of his clothes to get away from the woman. The wife claims Joseph attacked her, and this time he is imprisoned rather than tossed into a pit. But then Joseph the dreamer

///
What felt then like hurt and evil now looks much more like the birthplace of something brand new.
\\\

ends up interpreting dreams in jail, earns some credit, and winds up in the house of Pharaoh organizing resources on behalf of many people in the middle of famine, saving thousands of lives. In the end, his brothers come trying to get food, and after a few tricks and turns, Joseph is revealed as the leader he bragged about to his brothers way earlier. His family is reconciled and Joseph is able to say with great forgiveness and maturity: "You intended to harm me, but God intended it for good to accomplish what is now being done, the saving of many lives" (Genesis 50:20).

Much happens in the story that speaks to maturity, leadership, and the process that shapes an individual's gifts and our call. For our purposes, it is important to see that Joseph is able to grow from the time when one coat is stripped from him, to the time he chooses to leave his coat or cloak behind in order to flee a bad situation. The first one he brags about, which almost gets him killed. The second he runs from, toward another pit—a jail. In this process he gains the maturity to see how even evil, jealousy, and resentment don't sabotage the plans of God.

It is in this embrace of forgiveness that Joseph is able to live in the truth that evil in this world is not the determiner of reality. Even evil can't destroy the good. Joseph is able to say that God intended to use evil for good in order to save many. Joseph names his second child Ephraim, translated: "God made me fertile in the land of my affliction." Joseph's whole life is the story of people doing unforgettable, unfixable things that are somehow reshaped for Joseph's good.

When I left New Horizons and the kids I loved in 2009, it didn't feel like a happy ending. The organization had to grow beyond myself and other founding leaders. This birth process, for Linda and me being born into something new was long and painful. For the organization, it took time to move beyond the shadow of "old leaders." At times this led to painful experiences of hurt and unforgiveness that struck at the core of my relationships with the place I had served for most of my adult life. But looking back, regardless of what was done, I realize it became the catalyst to move me on. Looking back I can see what Joseph sees. Traveling and teaching, writing a book, and Linda launching Street Bean were all part of a painful process of birthing something new in me. The board and community that at some level hurt me were, to refer back to Lewis Smedes, just as confused and weak and human as I was, and they handled the transition no worse than I did.

What felt then like hurt and evil now looks much more like the birthplace of something brand new. Something that could only be delivered through pain. I have been able to see this now, and forgiveness accompanies the new vision. Joseph was able to reshape his story through forgiveness. He had the ability, in the end, to see God's plan in his own arrogance, his father's favoritism, and his broken brothers' unforgiven bitterness and jealousy. In this story we see a young man mature and develop new perceptions, and the capacity to extend grace and forgiveness.

SO WHAT DOES IT MEAN THAT IF WE DON'T FORGIVE WE WON'T BE FORGIVEN?

We will never really trust God's control and ability to act on our behalf if we hold too tightly to our view of justice, holding out for our way and our timing. Unforgiveness will blind us to the availability of God's forgiveness. If we cannot forgive, we cannot imagine living in forgiveness. We gain the assurance of God's forgiveness when we are able to practice it. We live either in forgiveness or unforgiveness. There is no in between. What we forgive is really gone, and what we are unable to forgive really sticks with us. And perhaps part of what Jesus is saying in the Book of Luke is that forgiveness is a powerful witness to the way of the Cross, as we join with Christ in saying: "Forgive them, for they do not know what they are doing" (Luke 23:34).

I started this chapter by telling you I was Pentecostal. As a Pentecostal, I grew up without knowing much about the church calendar or liturgy. But it's a part of church tradition I have grown to love. Liturgy is to the church service what the calendar is to the year. It creates active participation and rhythm. Pentecostal liturgies and calendars center me and help me participate in the story acted out in the life of the church. One regular part of the liturgy is the confession, where Christians as a community confess what they have done, usually followed by a time of silence, then a promise, an assurance of pardon. But, I have often wondered if this act of confession leading to assurance should be reversed. What if the assurance were first? Knowing you are forgiven, you are now empowered to confess. Ron Ruthruff is set free to act in forgiveness and set free to say, "I am sorry," because he is forgiven. With humility and honesty, forgiveness will change the world we live in. Every time I say I am sorry, I give someone the opportunity and the power to forgive. It is a form of me relinquishing control and giving away power to the other. This is an act of incredible justice in a world filled with resentment, judgement, bitterness, and blame. Forgiveness, both the request for forgiveness and the granting of forgiveness, is the interpersonal practice that could erode the scaffolding of systemic injustice. I think this is why Bishop Tutu continues to move in this spirit of forgiveness.

You are forgiven, so go and forgive, extending the same forgiveness to the world that you have learned to walk in, bearing witness to a great salvation. As you forgive, you will make more and more space to see for yourself God's power to heal, restore, and make all things new. Forgiveness is the first sign of the Resurrection.

CHAPTER 10

BEING SENT INTO THE WORLD

When the Son of Man comes in his glory, and all the angels with him, he will sit on his glorious throne. All the nations will be gathered before him, and he will separate the people one from another as a shepherd separates the sheep from the goats. He will put the sheep on his right and the goats on his left. Then the King will say to those on his right, "Come, you who are blessed by my Father; take your inheritance, the kingdom prepared for you since the creation of the world. For I was hungry and you gave me something to eat, I was thirsty and you gave me something to drink, I was a stranger and you invited me in, I needed clothes and you clothed me, I was sick and you looked after me, I was in prison and you came to visit me." Then the righteous will answer him, "Lord, when did we see you hungry and feed you, or thirsty and give you something to drink? When did we see you a stranger and invite you in, or needing clothes and clothe you? When did we see you sick or in prison and go to visit

you?" The King will reply, "Truly I tell you, whatever
you did for one of the least of these brothers and sisters of
mine, you did for me." Then he will say to those on his left,
"Depart from me, you who are cursed, into the eternal fire
prepared for the devil and his angels."

— MATTHEW 25:31–41

was recently invited to preach at Capitol Hill Presbyterian, a church in the center of Seattle. I have been there a few times and always felt the congregation had a great sense of curiosity and a willingness to engage their neighborhood, their city, and the world. Their pastor, James Kearny, asked me to preach on Matthew 25:31–43, the sheep and goats passage. It's a popular passage, I would argue almost as popular as the Good Samaritan story.

As I began to prepare for the sermon, it seemed like I could make a good go at it. For heaven's sake, I got the title for my first book, *The Least of These*, from this passage. But I did what I always do when I am given a text to speak on. Regardless of how much I think I know it, I begin to read it, and around it. When I say around, I mean literally *around* it. I read the verses that sit on either side of it and try to pay attention to what I might have missed in previous readings.

As I worked through the two or three chapters that precede the text, I began to wonder some about my previous readings. I began to think they had fallen short of the intention of the text. I felt like I had jumped to a popular conclusion that now, as I slowed down, didn't seem to speak to the complexity of the text. What precedes the text is a significant discourse in which Jesus really challenges the way the Pharisees are working out their religion in public. Woven into the story of the sheep and the goats is a message about the end of days — about who will be judged and what criteria they will be judged by.

I continue to believe this passage has significant social implications, that it is drawing our attention to those who have very little and are in desperate circumstances. But as I read backward and forward, I wondered if it was simply a statement about caring for the poor, homeless, imprisoned — the "least of these" in our culture — or if the passage had broader implications than my original reading had allowed. Maybe it had something more to say about being a follower of Jesus in the world.

The problem with reading the passage as a moral statement that says that those who love the least of these are "in" and those who don't are "out," I realized, is that it not only oversimplifies the theology around God's judgment and the end of all things but reveals a deep-seated tension between two faith traditions in the Christian church. These traditions, I argue, are cousins in the church, but neither will admit any family resemblance.

The holiness tradition, in an effort to shore up some sort of personal agency apart from formal church structures, established a form of spirituality that was shaped by personal piety and discipline. At its best, it allowed people to know that they were personally empowered as they followed Jesus. At its worst, the holiness tradition can quickly become an internal checklist built on private moral achievements.

On the other hand, the social justice tradition of the church is rightfully concerned with public morality. This tradition participated in the fight to end slavery and advocated for women's rights. But in the end, the moral imperative of the social justice stream can be just as dependent on public displays of justice as the holiness stream is committed to private morality.

///

Those who are sent out, who go hungry, who end up homeless, naked, and imprisoned, and those who have compassion for them, will be welcomed at the end of days.

**

These two streams could create balance in the church if they admitted the need for each other, but they both walk with a limp if they disregard each other. Neither tells the whole story of the Christian faith. Holiness at its weakest is only about personal piety; justice at its worst is only about what you do in public. The problem, then, with reading the sheep and goats chapter as if social justice alone gets you into heaven, is that the Gospels themselves challenge this concept simply by the way Jesus engages with perceived "insiders" and "outsiders." The Gospels don't present a story where good people help others, and the bad people are out of luck. What we find most often is that those who think of themselves as outside the kingdom are closer than they think, and those who think they have positioned themselves inside God's plan are not nearly as "in" as they imagined. Ethics are important in the life of a Christian, but moralism is not the only determiner in the outcome of the "last days."

Even if the passage *were* about judgment and the end of all things — what scholars call an apocalyptic or eschatological parable — that tells us who gets a reward and who gets punished, this message doesn't square with what we hear in the rest of Matthew's story. In Matthew 6:14–15, judgment is based on forgiveness — you will be forgiven in the same manner that you forgive. In 7:21, it's about obedience — do my Father's will and you will make it. Matthew 10:32 is about confession — acknowledge me, Jesus says, and I will acknowledge you. In 13:41, those who do evil will be judged. In 13:47–49, the kingdom of God is compared to a drag net that pulls up everything, and God and the angels are the ones who sort through the nets — not us. Later, in 16:27, we are promised that what you have done will dictate how you are judged, and in 19:28 the 12 tribes of Israel will be judged by Jesus' followers. Then in 24:13–14, we learn that those who endure to the end will be saved, and, finally, in 25:31–41, we are told that how you treat the least of these will be the measure by which the sheep are separated from the goats. At this point I found myself utterly confused. Maybe entering the kingdom wasn't about the least of these? Did I need to apologize for my first book's title? All in all, I decided, the final judgment seems to have a variety of criteria, the implication being that it's God's business to decide, and surely not mine. So, how do we move forward with this passage? What is the story really about?

///

As I mentioned, reading back into the chapters that precede the sheep and goats passage, one finds Jesus' intense criticisms of the Pharisees. Jesus obviously takes issue with the way they present themselves. He tells them in the middle of many "woes to you!" that while their tithe is significant, they have forgotten the more important matters of justice, mercy, and faithfulness (Matthew 23:23). Before this — just in case you were wondering who is in and who is out here — Jesus tell the religious leaders that the kingdom of God will be taken from them and given to the tax collectors and prostitutes (Matthew 21:31). Jesus then critiques the nature of the Pharisees' conversion and what they are converting others to, saying in 23:15, "You travel over land and sea to win a single convert, and when you have succeeded, you make them twice as much a child of hell as you are."

This is strong language. There is something about the behavior of the Pharisees and the beliefs they are pressing onto others that Jesus finds seriously problematic. The Pharisees have missed the most important things. The kingdom of God will be taken from them and given to those we least expect, people who seem to lack moral character. The Pharisees' message and method, while diligent, only produces and amplifies what they are: children of hell. This got me thinking. Jesus is critiquing the Pharisees' way of going out into the world and telling people about God. It reminded me of what some commentaries I had been reading about Matthew 25 say the passage of the sheep and goats may be about.

I had discovered that a significant portion of scholarly opinion on the passage brings into question how I had first read the text and affirmed my concerns. The problem seems to be with the phrase "all the nations," and the connection between the phrases "the least of these" and "my brothers and sisters." What I found was that folks who know the Bible way better than I do seem to think that this is what the passage is about: Jesus' "brothers and sisters" could be referring to the followers being sent into uncharted territory, to "all the nations," now gathered before the throne.

The more I read, the more I asked, could this be Jesus defending His disciples, who He will send to unfamiliar places where they will be treated poorly, go hungry, and find themselves naked and imprisoned? Maybe this really isn't a simple moral statement about the criteria for final judgment being how you treated marginalized people.

I began to wonder, what if this is a *sending passage*? What if Jesus is talking in Matthew 25 to His followers, contrasting the way the Pharisees go out into the world with the way He sends His followers out? Maybe He is cautioning and comforting them as He sends them out past all the limits of their culture and religion, far beyond their comfort zone, with these words: those who are sent out, who go hungry, who end up homeless, naked, and imprisoned, and those who have compassion for them, will be welcomed at the end of days, but their oppressors will face judgment. Because in mistreating the bearers of Jesus' message, you mistreat Jesus Himself. If this is what the passage is saying, for me the question becomes, how does Jesus ask His followers to go out into the world in contrast to what the Pharisees are doing — and why does it end so badly for them? As I explored that question, I discovered that the way Jesus sends His disciples in the Gospels is simple and profound, and speaks to justice, mercy, and humility.

In the Gospel of John, Jesus simply says He is sending His disciples out in the same way His Father sent him:

> *Again Jesus said, "Peace be with you! As the Father has sent me, I am sending you."*
>
> —JOHN 20:21

In Matthew, we get a retelling of a sending passage from Isaiah 42:

> *Here is my servant whom I have chosen, the one I love, in whom I delight; I will put my Spirit on him, and he will proclaim justice to the nations. He will not quarrel or cry out; no one will hear his voice in the streets. A bruised*

reed he will not break, and a smoldering wick he will not
snuff out, till he has brought justice through to victory. In
his name the nations will put their hope.

— MATTHEW 12:18–21

In Matthew 18:4, Jesus tells His disciples that unless they turn and become lowly like children, they will never enter the kingdom of God. In Luke 10, Jesus sends them out and tells them to take nothing with them. Odd advice. Even more strange, back in Matthew 10:16, He sends them out as sheep among wolves, trusting that hospitality will be offered to them. Let's recap: Jesus sends out His disciples like He Himself has been sent. They are, like Him, called to proclaim justice, and be a signpost of hope. But the manner in which they go will need to look a lot more childlike. They must be innocent and vulnerable.

So Jesus' followers are told to go out as children, as sheep, carrying nothing. They are to extend mercy and place themselves in communities with nothing at their disposal, making themselves incredibly vulnerable — maybe more vulnerable than those they serve. This speaks of incredible solidarity. They are called to fully share in the very humanness and vulnerability of the communities and the homes they enter. This sounds a lot like the way Jesus came to us. They are to begin to act out the story of God in such a way that brings righteousness and justice together.

///

If I cannot go out in the
way of Jesus, I should not go out
in the name of Jesus.

****

At no time in history is going in the way of Jesus — vulnerable, gentle, and merciful — more important than right now. Living in a postmodern world, many of us Western

Christians have attempted to assimilate our faith, revelation, and inspiration to the modern world of the Enlightenment. At the risk of oversimplification, we've tried to push faith into discrete scientific categories

///

Power and privilege don't mix well with a religion whose most definitive moment revolves around a tool used to publicly execute rebels of the state.

\\\

that are much too small. But when we try to prove our faith through the scientific method, we paint ourselves into a theological and philosophical corner. I believe it was a mistake for much of the church to follow in the trail of the Enlightenment and build its apologetic on the scientific premise of what can be known through reason and analysis. Because as science explores what can be known, it also reveals more and more of what cannot be known. If our faith does the same thing, we find ourselves limited to what we think we can prove, and unable to speak to the mystery that is faith. This has produced a crisis within the church, in which we are trying to reduce inspiration and revelation to scientific formulas. Needing that kind of certainty is incredibly limiting, and doesn't really work. When truth is pushed into this scientific corner, faith becomes its first casualty.

In addition to this crisis, as globalization has brought the human community much closer and we have begun to see that there are ways of believing and knowing outside Western tradition, we are confronted with the reality that there is an ever-expanding marketplace of competing ideas. We live in a postmodern society in which worlds are colliding and belief systems are shaped based on where one comes from and where one is currently located. In this new emerging world, if we are honest, we don't know why we believe some of what we hold as true. This is a postmodern world

///

If we stand with the least of these in the manner that Jesus stood with them, we will also experience all the meanness this world has in store for them.

\\\

in which we can no longer *prove* what we believe. I am convinced the best response is to once again rely on faith. The advice of Jesus to take nothing with you for the journey, with all humility, is the only way to step out into the world of competing ideologies. It could be that in this world the Christian can no longer claim: "I know, and I believe," but rather, the much more humble and open-ended "I don't know, but I believe." This I would consider a faith-filled posture. One dependent not on fact, but on a deep faith in the desire of the Almighty to reveal Himself to the creation He loves.

We not only live in a postmodern world. We live in a postcolonial world. This does not mean that racism, xenophobia, and imperialism are dead. They are not, and they still impact all our global interactions. But in a postcolonial world, we are beginning to be made aware of the consequences and implications of the Western colonial takeover, and how imbedded our faith was in this movement.[1] Many thought they went into the New World by the power of the Spirit. Only recently have we realized we went in the spirit of the West. We thought we took Jesus to people who needed Him, but often we took only a gospel of assimilation and patriarchal relationships. In this world, we must learn to take less with us. Or, better said, to be aware of what we take. Power and privilege don't mix well with a religion whose most definitive moment revolves around a tool used to publicly execute rebels of the state. This Cross is our symbol. Our God came to us in the flesh, a traveling carpenter, with no place to be born, no place to live, and no place to be buried.

The implication of this sending passage in Matthew 25 is, if we go in the way of Jesus, we should expect to be treated as He was as He constantly welcomed those who sit on the edges of the community, outside of what is perceived as clean, pure, and good. If we extend mercy to law breakers and proclaim that justice has everything to do with righteousness, if we take nothing with us and sit in solidarity with those who live where we have been sent, we will experience all that they do: isolation, hunger, homelessness, and suffering. If we stand with the least of these in the manner that Jesus stood with them, we will also experience all the meanness this world has in store for them. I realize this doesn't sound like good news. But it does sound like Jesus saying, if they persecuted Me, they will persecute you (John 15:20). Don't be surprised. In this world you will have trouble (16:33).

Jesus asks us to live into a profoundly vulnerable identification with the world around us that I, for one, most often want to say, "No, thank you" to. But I am also more and more convinced that if I cannot go out in the way of Jesus, I should not go out in the name of Jesus. I don't know if I want to cross the road to get close enough to feel the pain of those who are beaten, robbed, and left for dead. I don't want to enter another's pain, and I sure don't want to enter into my own. But I also know that while there is nothing wrong with acts of mercy, left to themselves, these acts never redistribute power. Acts of mercy are different than the way of mercy. Justice demands we ask for all our brothers and sisters to be viewed and treated

///

We overcome by letting go and dying to the fabricated mechanisms that keep us propped up, the systems that are really just illusions of power and control.

****

as image bearers of God. The solidarity that leads to justice is in taking a posture in the world that relinquishes a ministry of simple acts of kindness that keeps us helping and keeps the vulnerable in need of help. The way of Jesus is a deeply incarnational, human approach. His example of justice asks us to enter into the same pain the world experiences, admit to the same fears, die to the same grandiose ideas we all have, lament over what isn't right, and enter into the counterintuitive journey toward the Cross.

What will sustain us if we live in this mercy, justice, and solidarity? Jesus said in this world we would have trouble, but He also encourages us to "Take heart! I have overcome the world" (John 16:33). We overcome by actually believing that the way of Jesus has conquered the way of the world. We overcome by letting go and dying to the fabricated mechanisms that keep us propped up, the systems that are really just illusions of power and control. And only by entering into this kind of death can the hope of the Resurrection be realized.

We will only have the courage to be sent in this way if we remember. Remember we are part of a story that claims that some trust in chariots and horses, but we trust in the name of the Lord. We remember that those who go out weeping will return with songs of joy. I think we do have to ask ourselves honestly, as we go out in the way of Jesus, do we really believe and trust in the Resurrection? Resurrection not as escapism, but as a faith-filled catalyst that sends us with trusting assurance back into the world, entering into our own and our neighbor's suffering, knowing that we have already overcome the world through Christ as we enter back into all that we as humans have tried to escape. Do we know that in bearing these crosses comes resurrection?

I STILL BELIEVE IN THE RESURRECTION

I walked down a long narrow path through a cemetery behind the casket of a sixteen-year-old Guatemalan street boy. I was speaking at a consultation for street kid organizations, churches, and city officials in Guatemala City, where in the same week, a beautiful young man had been gunned down. The conference was ended early, and many of us went to walk with some of the street kids in the community as they buried their friend. As I followed the kids along the path, I was struck by the enormous cemetery and how easy it was to identify where the rich were laid to rest and the poor were buried. The rich placed their loved ones in houses made of stone, accentuated with sculptures; they looked like mausoleums. The poor were stacked in wooden caskets five stories high in morgue-type concrete containers. They looked like safety deposit boxes. As we followed the casket, people sold soda pop and snacks along the way. Death must be common in Guatemala. Funeral processions were a captive audience for social enterprise.

We got to the outer reaches of the cemetery, and the sound of weeping increased. A few strong boys lifted the wooden box that held their friend onto a machine that hoisted the casket two rows up. The priest began the funeral mass in Spanish, and I walked a respectful distance away to give space to those who knew the boy being memorialized. I was only a few feet from the gathering when I noticed, over the embankment, there seemed to be a make-shift garbage dump down a long steep hill. In it lay the fragments of many caskets similar to the one being lifted up into the square opening. After the service ended, I asked my friend Joel, "What's the story with all the unused caskets?" They were being broken, crushed, and pushed aside by the blade of a bull dozer into pile a few yards away. "Oh those aren't unused caskets," he said with little affect. "None of the poor can afford to buy a spot in the cemetery. They rent these spaces for maybe a year or two, then when they run out of money, the space is rented to someone else. The casket is pulled out and tossed over the cliff." This street boy, I realized, who had no home in life, had no home in death either. It was a rented space. Even in death he would be evicted and tossed away.

///

This street boy, I realized, who had no home in life, had no home in death either.

**

As I looked over the edge at a pile of broken boards that had once been caskets, I thought of another story of One who had no place to be buried. A borrowed tomb became His resting place. But before He died, He made a bold promise: "My Father's house has many rooms; if that were not so, would I have told you that I am going there to prepare a place for you?" (John 14:2).

I wondered if I believed in this resurrection hope for the boy and all the others whose caskets were now being crushed into kindling. Did I believe it for them, and more honestly, did I believe it for myself? What does this belief produce in me? Does it launch me into the afterlife so completely that I am no earthly good, avoiding all the hard places in the world in hope of a sweet by-and-by? Did I only believe in the Resurrection as a metaphor that smooths over the lonely, difficult places in this world with a Pollyanna-ish change of perspective? Or did I believe in the physical resurrection initiated by Jesus that will make all things new for all of us? Somehow as I reflected on this, I wondered if, rather than pushing me away from the world, what if, like Jesus, the Resurrection pushed me back into the world?

Could the hope of the Resurrection cause me to live differently, to honestly enter into my own suffering and the suffering in the world? Could it be an assurance in moments that feel like death and despair? If I really believe this, I thought, rather than avoid pain, suffering, and death, perhaps I would have the courage to move back toward the dreadful things in the world and the dreadful things in myself, knowing that resurrection is found in the middle of those things. Knowing that by entering into the dreadful things, one bears witness to the new life of God in the world. Can we enter into all that is broken in this world, knowing that there is a place for us promised in Scripture? Can we choose death in spite of fear in the hope of life? Can we love the world to the point of death, knowing that we are simply following Jesus as we do, and

///

This Resurrection should cause me to live differently in the world. It should cause me to live closer to the edge.

**

that the way to the Resurrection is through the darkest places in ourselves and in the world we live in?

If I believe in this death and this Resurrection of Jesus, I must believe that there is a place for me and the street boy and all those who no longer occupy the kindling that was once caskets that now lay below me. This Resurrection should cause me to live differently in the world. It should cause me to live closer to the edge.

THE CHURCH AT EPHESUS

Be completely humble and gentle; be patient, bearing with one another in love. Make every effort to keep the unity of the Spirit through the bond of peace. There is one body and one Spirit, just as you were called to one hope when you were called.

— EPHESIANS 4:2–4

When I think about this letter written to the church in Ephesus, I am struck by these verses. They seem to be a thesis or centerpiece of the correspondence. This is a community that believes and lives as if they are marked with the seal of the resurrected spirit of Jesus (Ephesians 1:13–14). They believed in the Resurrection of Jesus as a promise they could count on. They behaved as if this resurrection was more real than their own lives, and it changed the way they lived their lives.

In John 20:19, we see Jesus in His resurrected body entering a locked room where His disciples waited. Rather than think of Jesus in terms of ghost or spirit, some fluffy, Casper-type entity, what if the Resurrection is more real that the lives we live? I know very little about science, but I do know that matter can penetrate matter that is less dense than itself. Maybe Jesus is more real in the Resurrection than the walls and locked doors He seemed to magically pass through.

C. S. Lewis creates this same imagery when a character in *The Great Divorce* steps on blades of grass in heaven that hurt his feet. Lewis's implication is that heaven is more real than the physical bodies we currently find ourselves in. This is the hope that holds this community in Ephesus together. They are so marked by the Resurrection, they so believed this story, that it caused them to live into a peace and a gentleness that was evident to the world around them. They knew that the powers of this world were not the final judge of what we have hope in, and they lived accordingly.

How did this hope express itself in their community? The text says they were a group of people who were confident in the fact that they were chosen by Christ (1:4), marked with the seal of the Spirit (1:13), and foreigners brought close (2:12–13). In their identity as chosen people, they realized that through Jesus, God had chosen them not for their own sake, but to be a blessing to others. The idea that the gift of God is for all people is all over the letter (2:6–7, 11–22; 3:6). They were chosen by God, not for their own sake, but to do good work and exemplify God's love in the world (2:10).

This love is a risky, honest practice and probably messier than any of us want to admit. The love the Ephesians were asked to bear witness to in the world was grace — unmerited and unearned favor. Grace is either free or it is not grace.

///

Beliefs don't dictate how we live; values do. Beliefs are what we say is true. Values are what we act on.

**

163

This love is a practical one. It speaks truth in love (4:15). This love doesn't slander (4:31) but rather subjects itself in mutual submission (5:21). And it works hard (4:28).

I believe this community of followers in the ancient city of Ephesus offer a good example of how we are to live in the world. They were a group of people who were chosen by sheer grace and entrusted with the good news that God's desire is to unite all creation unto God's self. This grace was a gift for the sake of the world — they had no room to brag about it. This community so counted on the hope found in Jesus' Resurrection, they lived and loved like their lives depended on it. Because they did. This was the value that shaped their community and their witness to the world around them.

VALUES, BELIEFS, AND LIFESTYLE

Then Jesus said to his disciples: "Therefore I tell you, do not worry about your life, what you will eat; or about your body, what you will wear. For life is more than food, and the body more than clothes. . . . Consider how the wild flowers grow. They do not labor or spin. Yet I tell you, not even Solomon in all his splendor was dressed like one of these. If that is how God clothes the grass of the field . . . how much more will he clothe you — you of little faith! And do not set your heart on what you will eat or drink . . . For the pagan world runs after all such things, and your Father knows that you need them. But seek his kingdom, and these things will be given to you as well. Do not be afraid, little flock, for your Father has been pleased to give you the kingdom. Sell your possessions

and give to the poor. Provide purses for yourselves that
will not wear out, a treasure in heaven that will never
fail, where no thief comes near and no moth destroys.
For where your treasure is, there your heart will be also."

—LUKE 12:22–34

I have always told my students we should spend time in the biblical text not only in places that bring us comfort and joy, but also in places that we have a clear aversion to. This is one of those texts. It seems absolutely impossible. Sell you possessions, give alms, and make purses that don't wear out. For those who claim that the Bible is always clear and definitive, this is a dangerous text. And it's not just found in this Luke 12 — it is a theme all over the Gospels. (See Matthew 6:19 and 19:21, Mark 10:21, Luke 12:13–15, 14:33 and 18:22–23.)

Jesus' words are simple. Where your treasure is — that is where you heart is going to be. Said a bit differently, beliefs don't dictate how we live; values do. Beliefs are what we say is true. Values are what we act on. Whatever you value is going to be exemplified in how you live. Where we live and how we spend our time and money tells us a lot more about what we really think is true than what we say we believe. Where you treasure is — what you value — is where your heart will be — where your life will be spent.

No place is this more evident than in marriage. I am not a great counselor, but on occasion I have had the opportunity to spend time with couples prior to their wedding and then officiate the wedding. If I am included in this process, I always request a follow up with coffee and conversation a few months after the ceremony. At this point, it is no shock to me how, after being married for six months or a year, most couples are grappling with their values, beliefs, and lifestyle. But the surprise for me is how quickly what they declared to be their beliefs seem to fall away once they began living together. What each person actually values makes a much bigger difference. So Christian couples claiming a very similar belief system are now sitting in utter frustration with their partner because what they value — and thus how they live — looks shockingly different.

This is true of me as well. After completing my doctorate, I realized I had been sitting. Constantly sitting. I was a bit fatter than I wanted to be. I kept saying that I valued losing weight and eating healthy, but I didn't lose a pound. What I believed was that I should lose weight. What I really valued was potatoes. My body and life carried the resemblance of what I valued over what I believed. My doctor, in his brilliance, told me about an incredible, sure-fire weight loss plan, and I quickly told him I was in: "Exercise more and eat less!" was his brilliant expert advice. This concept had to become more valuable to me than a hamburger, and what I valued would literally be exemplified in how my heart and belly looked.

Jesus gets to the core of what keeps us tethered to values that hold us back from living in the radical freedom of storing our treasures in heaven. Jesus tells His audience to sell their possessions. New Testament scholar N. T. Wright, in *Jesus and the Victory of God*, observes that Jesus is talking about wealth in the context of land — land that in an agrarian culture shaped identity and created security. Jesus is really asking His audience, and us, to give up those things that keep us secure and inform who we are. This to me is terrifying.

///

The places that look most dead in our world carry the most potential for life.

****

DON'T WORRY, YOU'RE GONNA DIE

Of course the story goes on. Jesus knows that His challenge will expose the anxiety that is at the root of this behavior of accumulation. Jesus tells His listeners not to worry in verse 25, but it's not "don't worry, you'll be fine"; rather, it's "don't worry you're going to die." Birds die, lilies and grass die, and so will you. Jesus gets to the heart of the issue by telling all of us that no matter how we try to hang on to our identities and struggle for security, in the end we die. In the Gospel of Luke, Jesus reveals something in all of us, our motivation for control: we are afraid.

I love the film *Moonstruck*. Linda and I watch it for our anniversary or Valentine's Day every year. It is the story of love. Loretta, played by Cher, has had some bad luck. Her first husband was killed by a bus. As she gets a bit older, she begins to wonder if she should settle. Should she marry out of the practical reality that she's not getting any younger, or should she hold out for love? If you have watched the film, you know that love sneaks up on her, and it is complicated. Olympia Dukakis plays Loretta's mother, Rose Castorini. She is the matriarch of a New York Italian family. She is beautiful and knows who she is. Her husband, Cosmo, is having an affair, and Rose spends most of the film trying to affirm her hunch and figure out why men cheat. She asks several people, but the answers don't confirm her gut sense. At the end of the film, when Loretta dumps Johnny Cammareri for his risky, younger brother Ronny, Rose asks the safe and dull Johnny why men have affairs. He confirms what she has known all along. He says it's because they fear death. *Exactly*. The patriarch of this beautiful and complex family must face what we all face. No matter how much we pretend we are young and powerful, like the birds and the lilies, we should accept that we are frail and we will die.

Luke Timothy Johnson explains it well, in *The Writings of the New Testament: An Interpretation,* when he says nothing we do can protect us from death. Life is fragile. Even if the birds and flowers toiled, it wouldn't help them. The choice is between trying to be in control and allowing what we own to shape our identities, or accepting that these things do us no good. The question Johnson sees Jesus posing is this: do we live like we have to control all that sustains us, or do we trust in the eternal plan of God?

MAKE PURSES THAT WILL LAST

> What we know about our beginnings and our end-
> ings, then, creates a different kind of present tense
> for us. We can live according to an ethic whereby we
> are not driven, controlled, anxious, frantic, or greedy,
> precisely because we are sufficiently at home and at
> peace to care about others as we have been cared for.
>
> —WALTER BRUEGGEMANN, *DEEP MEMORY, EXUBERANT HOPE*

I love what Brueggemann is saying in the quotation above. We can only be fully present — free from anxiety — if we have a clear sense of where we come from and where we are going. I believe the key to this truth sits in Luke 12:32: "Do not be afraid, little flock, for your Father has been pleased to give you the kingdom."

Brendan Byrne claims that this is better translated not "your Father has been pleased" but "your Father is determined" in his book, *The Hospitality of God.* What if we really believed God will take care of us? Maybe not in the fashion we expected, but what if we really lived as if we trusted our beginnings and endings to a God who is determined to take care of us? I argue that if we did, we would be able to enter into the hardest places in our own lives and the hardest places in the world with courage, confidence, and a humble understanding that through the Resurrection, the kingdom of God, regardless of what we see right now, is moving toward us at such a breakneck pace we couldn't stop it if we wanted to.

> *For now we see only a reflection as in a mirror; then we shall see face to face. Now I know in part; then I shall know fully, even as I am fully known.*
>
> —1 CORINTHIANS 13:12

The Resurrection tells me I can live beyond fear, control, and rivalry, and that, in fact, we cannot live into the Resurrection controlled by these things, but rather by faith, hope, and love.

Can we embrace the hope that those who go out weeping will return with joy? We live in a world in which, usually, the more we have, the less we give. We live in a world that seems to believe that the one who dies with the most toys or degrees wins. But can we be people that so believe that God is determined to take care of us that we enter into the painful story of the world? Can we be people who strive to believe it? Some days, honestly, I don't. Other days, parts of me die, and it hurts, but I always see in those times a little of the resurrection. It's like my wife's compost pile. I believe that all the dead grass and wilted flowers and food scraps that look like garbage are producing new life. The places that look most dead in our world carry the most potential for life.

One morning, recently, I walked out of the train tunnel like every other day. The homeless man I had known as the skinny, mentally ill boy at New Horizons was sitting in the entrance again, and we made eye contact. This time he wasn't crying or moaning. He was clean and in his right mind. He looked at me, and the expression on his face confirmed that he knew me. It had been at least 25 years since we had spoken. I called out his name, "Scott," and he looked back at me, smiled, and said "Ron!" He said it had been a long time and asked me what I was doing. I told him I was a professor at The Seattle School of Theology and Psychology. "Well," he joked, "I might stop by and visit, 'cause I need some psychology and theology!" He laughed and I laughed. In that moment I felt the Resurrection, at least some small picture of it. There was a moment when I could see beyond a broken boy and homeless man and into the soul of a fellow human being. I knew his name and he knew mine, and that moment felt like a glimpse of what it would be like when all things were good and complete. I felt the hope that in the middle of things being human and broken, something new had just shown up, and it felt worth believing in. I didn't want to go to heaven in that moment. I wanted to go further into the world. I had seen a glimpse of the way things should be and the way things are going to be and it was worth gambling on again.

> *He who was seated on the throne said, "I am making everything new!" Then he said, "Write this down, for these words are trustworthy and true."*
>
> —REVELATION 21:5

DISCUSSION QUESTIONS

Chapter 1   The City is My Teacher, the World My Classroom

What are the biggest challenges in your community?

Describe the assets you could identify to address these challenges.

In what way do these challenges and assets reveal the best and the worst in you?

Chapter 2   Lament

How have you lived in denial when your problems seemed too much to bear?

What are the mechanisms of covert despair at work in your life, and what ways have you rerouted denial?

What things about your own life and the lives of others in your community do you need to take the time to grieve?

How might it benefit hurting people to resist the impulse to fix things and simply "feel" with them?

Chapter 3   Setting a Different Table,
Creating Space for the Other

In what ways have fear and control limited your ability to invite others to a table of community?

What does Mary give up in relinquishing the role of host in her own home?

What does she gain by letting her guest, Jesus, guide the interaction?

As people of faith, what do we hang on to and what can we let go of as we set a bigger table?

How do believers embody this bigger table?

Chapter 4   Finding Where the Kingdom Grows

What needs to be tilled up in you to enable the kingdom to grow?

In the past week, where did you see the kingdom pop up in a place or at a time you least expected?

How do we cultivate a kingdom of God that grows in ways and places that we might not expect?

Chapter 5   Really Good Reasons Not to Give

What are good reasons not to give?

What does it mean for you to go to the other side of the road?

Describe a time you helped someone and were surprised by a lesson you learned.

Chapter 6   Loving Mercy, Doing Justice

Why is there such a struggle between justice and righteousness?

On which end of the spectrum do you fall?

What could be learned from the other side?

What does justice and mercy look like when it is lived out in a community?

Chapter 7   Following Jesus in the Way of the Cross

Has your community been overly influenced by the idea of victory?

Does the message of the Cross invite all believers into a new way of living in the world?

How can you die to yourself without self-deprecation or codependency?

If the Cross tells the truth, what would it expose in your community?

Chapter 8   Where Are You Willing to Go?

Describe a time in your life when you felt like you were in wilderness or exile.

In this place of exile, how did the journey shape you spiritually?

How did solitude help shape the experience?

What did you need from community during this time?

Chapter 9 Forgiveness Sets Them, and Us, Free

What is the most difficult part of giving and receiving forgiveness?

How can you apply forgiveness in situations that need a just response for victims of traumatic actions?

Do unforgiveness, resentment, and bitterness give a sense of power?

Does forgiveness provide freedom from the past?

How could actively giving and receiving forgiveness lead to a more just world?

Chapter 10   Being Sent Into the World

What would it look like to embrace the kingdom of God as a child?

What would it look like to take the posture of lambs among wolves for justice's sake?

If Jesus is telling believers to humbly serve the least of these, what does this solidarity with the afflicted look like?

Chapter 11 *I Still Believe in the Resurrection*

In what ways have believers used the Resurrection as a way to escape the challenges of this world?

How could the promise of Resurrection change the way present-day believers live, like it changed the church at Ephesus?

What would it look like to believe in the Resurrection in a way that gives believers back to the world as agents of change?

NOTES

Chapter 1

1. These ideas were first presented at a Street Psalms intensive titled *City of Joy*. The Street Psalms community is the community in which I am an ordained clergy, and the Street Psalms intensives are a series of theological trainings for young leaders serving youth and families in hard places. Much of the thinking for this book has been cultivated in my deep friendships with the Street Psalms Community.

2. From Jon Abe's presentation to an urban studies course for Northwest University. Jon is the director of Youth Detention Chaplaincy at Urban Impact, a community development organization serving in the Rainier Valley neighborhood of Seattle.

3. William Finnegan, *Cold New World: Growing up in a Harder America* (New York, NY: Modern Library, 1998), 269–340. Finnegan points out that the Antelope Valley is a community who fled the city for independence and anonymity. 45% of students who entered high school didn't graduate, 50% of youth were unsupervised after school. In one year only 6 of 400 graduating seniors went to University of California School, the higher tier of public educational and 10% of gradates went to any college at all. The Antelope Valley is the story of families fleeing the dangers of Los Angeles only to discover the same problems in the community they ran to.

4.   Dominique DuBois Gillard, "The Unbearable Whiteness of Being: Part of Setting the Captive Free is Helping People See the Invisible Bonds of Structural Racism," *Sojourners*, April 2015.

5.   Jeffery Sachs, *The End of Poverty: Economic Possibilities for Our Time* (New York, NY: Penguin Books, 2005). Sachs argues that a lack of cross-border relationships is a leading cause of developing countries remaining entrenched in poverty. My argument is that we see the same dynamic in our own neighborhoods as well.

Chapter 2

1.   The lament actually brings to the surface the very things that are so painful we are prone to simply deny or shove from our memory. Lament calls them from our soul and forces us to declare them as forces that shape our belief about ourselves and about God.

Chapter 3

1.   David Bohm, *On Dialogue* (New York, NY: Routledge Classic, 1996). This idea was formulated as I read Bohm's book. This little book speaks to how to engage in discourse. While it is has no sense of Christian spirituality, it feels directly connected to Nouwen's idea of hospitality.

Chapter 4

1. John Dominic Crossan, *Jesus: A Revolutionary Biography* (New York, NY: HarperOne, 1994), 64–66.

Chapter 7

1. Douglas John Hall, *The Cross in Our Context: Jesus and the Suffering World* (Minneapolis, MI: Fortress Press, 2003), 14.

Chapter 8

1. This journey with street kids from outreach on the street to the beginnings of the coffee shop where street youth were hired into the coffee industry can be found in my first book, *The Least of These: Lessons Learned From Kids on the Street*, New Hope Publishers, 2010.

2. My reading of this text is dependent on a conversation Bill Moyers has with an interfaith panel in his public television series, that has been transcribed in the companion book to the series titled, *Genesis: A Living Conversation* (New York, NY: Doubleday, 1996), 219–247.

Chapter 10

1. For a more comprehensive treatment of these observations that I have only touched on, read *The Christian Imagination: Theology and the Origins of Race* by Willie James Jennings and *Transforming Mission: Paradigm Shifts in Theology and Mission* by David J Bosch.

New Hope® Publishers is a division of WMU®, an international organization that challenges Christian believers to understand and be radically involved in God's mission. For more information about WMU, go to wmu.com. More information about New Hope books may be found at NewHopePublishers.com. New Hope books may be purchased at your local bookstore.

Use the QR reader on your
smartphone to visit us online at
NewHopePublishers.com

If you've been blessed by this book, we would like to hear your story. The publisher and author welcome your comments and suggestions at: newhopereader@wmu.org.

Resources for
Upside-Down Living!

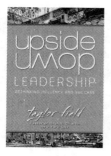

Upside-Down Leadership

Rethinking Influence
and Success

TAYLOR FIELD

ISBN-13: 978-1-59669-342-5
N124147• $14.99

Upside-Down Freedom

Inverted Principles
for Christian Living

TAYLOR FIELD

ISBN-13: 978-1-59669-376-0
N134117• $14.99

Upside-Down Results

God Tags People for
His Purposes

SUSAN FIELD

ISBN-13: 978-1-59669-404-0
N144110 • $14.99

Upside-Down Devotion

Extreme Action for a
Remarkable God

TAYLOR FIELD

ISBN 13: 978-1-59669-405-7
N144111 • $14.99

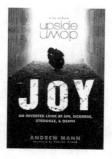

Upside-Down Joy

An Inverted Look at Sin,
Sickness, Struggle, & Death

ANDREW MANN

ISBN 13: 978-1-59669-440-8
N154118 • $14.99

**To learn more about this series, visit NewHopePublishers.com.
Available in bookstores everywhere.**